1.50

New Jersey

Haunted New Jersey

Ghosts and Strange Phenomena
of the Garden State

Patricia A. Martinelli
and Charles A. Stansfield Jr.

STACKPOLE
BOOKS

Published by
STACKPOLE BOOKS
5067 Ritter Road
Mechanicsburg, PA 17055
www.stackpolebooks.com

Printed in the United States of America

10 9 8 7 6 5 4 3

FIRST EDITION

Illustrations by Heather Adel
Cover design by Caroline Stover

There is no doubt in our minds that there are even more stories about the Garden State's ghostly inhabitants, which we hope to include in another volume. If you have any tales that you would like to share, any close encounters that you would care to relate, please feel free to contact the authors at HauntedNJ2004@wmconnect.com.

Library of Congress Cataloging-in-Publication Data

Martinelli, Patricia A.
    Haunted New Jersey : ghosts and strange phenomena of the Garden
  State / Patricia A. Martinelli and Charles A. Stansfield, Jr.
        p.   cm.
    Includes bibliographical references.
    ISBN 0-8117-3156-1 (pbk.)
    1. Ghosts–New Jersey.   2. Monsters–New Jersey.   I. Stansfield,
  Charles A.   II. Title.
  BF1472.U6 M38   2004
  133.1'09749–dc22

                                                            2003023431

  ISBN 978-0-8117-3156-0

Contents

Contents

Introduction

WHAT SCARES YOU?

Is it the creak of footsteps on nonexistent stairs? The whisper of voices in an empty room? What about the silent figure of a woman gliding down a shadowy hallway one moment, only to be gone the next? The experience of a sudden, inexplicable chill?

Are there such things as ghosts? Does the supernatural world occasionally overlap with ours, allowing ethereal creatures to move from one plane of existence to the next?

Spirits and monsters, as well as travelers from other worlds, apparently have haunted humankind for generations; legends and traditions of ghosts and unearthly creatures are common to virtually all cultures and peoples. Most psychologists would say these beings are simply another face for our inner emotional turmoil; they are an expression of fears we cannot otherwise confront. Many scientists would declare that such creatures cannot be scientifically observed or documented and, therefore, are not worth worrying about. While valid arguments against the existence of the paranormal can usually be made by experts in various fields, even the most hardened cynic often will admit to at least one inexplicable experience and pause when hearing something go bump in the night.

Internationally renowned ghost expert Hans Holzer, in *Yankee Ghosts,* summarized the general understanding of ghosts this way:

"Ghosts are people, or parts of people, anyway, and are governed by emotional stimuli. It is not always easy for a ghost to tell his tale, for he is like a psychotic. We are dealing with the emotional memory of a person who has died under tragic circumstances and keeps reliving those final moments over and over, unaware that death, as we know it, has occurred." Spirits make their presence known in a variety of ways, from materializing unexpectedly to moving furniture. Legendary creatures can appear suddenly without warning: often they seem as surprised by us as we are by them. Despite reports of such incidents, however, not everyone readily accepts the existence of a supernatural world. Some researchers feel it is necessary to collect more substantial data. Although there frequently is only tainted, suspect hard evidence, they come lavishly equipped with cameras, radar, and motion detectors and devote a great deal of time and resources to investigating phenomena ranging from UFOs to the Loch Ness Monster. Why? These people have accepted the possibility that such heretofore undocumented creatures *could* exist. As it is patently impossible to prove that something *cannot* be, probably the researchers, like the majority of people, are open to speculation about the unknown.

Academics have also studied and described in detail the various physical, cultural, and historical qualities of places. Nearly everyone, whatever their level of education and expertise, has experienced, with some unease, an occasional scary sense of place that is unusual and special. No specific incident or phenomenon need be ingrained in memory, just a vague awareness of an unusual quality of place, perhaps unattributable to any particular observation or sensory input. Except for actual sightings of apparitions, the experience often is sensed on a different level of awareness. Although visitors to a region are sometimes skeptical about the local haunted house or cemetery, residents may take a hands-off approach to the area. They may profess not to believe, but that doesn't mean they're going to take any unnecessary chances.

Conventional social pressures may suggest that a person not freely communicate to others this fleeting, somewhat indescribable prickling of the senses. But at a primal stratum of the brain, the memory lingers, to be recalled suddenly by another's ghost or demon story. The reaction, even when the words aren't spoken out loud is, "Yes! I've felt that, too!" And so our fascination with ghost stories and monsters continues, even among professed nonbelievers.

New Jersey has had its share of supernatural sightings. Witches have been known to roam the night, performing centuries-old rituals to unlock magical secrets. And for generations, myths and legends have been handed down involving ghosts and monsters that "live" everywhere from urban high-rise hotels to the wilds of the Pine Barrens. These creatures have both frightened and entertained us in bedtime stories, books, and movies. This book will attempt to bring many of these tales together for a unique tour through the Garden State. Whether or not you're a believer, enter here and maybe, just maybe, you will find out once and for all . . . What scares you?

A Brief History of Ghosts and Legends

Every culture, dating to ancient China, has written and oral records of encounters with ghosts and supernatural beings, both good and evil. In the third century B.C., a long-divided China was unified under its first emperor, Chin, a warrior deemed to be literally the "son of the dragon" because this awesome but benevolent creature provided him with superior strength, intelligence, and all the other positive qualities needed in a true leader. To the Chinese people, the dragon was a rarely glimpsed but extremely real creature. However, while dragons and some other creatures (which were eventually dubbed mythological) were respected, the Chinese feared ghosts. Restless spirits were believed to be unhappy because they were unfairly trapped in this dimension, and they would punish family members accordingly for their pain.

The Egyptians, with their elaborate funerary procedures for the upper class, also feared the ghosts of their dead. This was one reason so much effort was made to placate them and provide them with creature comforts when they crossed into the afterlife. Many later European cultures, including the Vikings, also attempted to appease spirits in this fashion.

When Christianity first flourished in Europe, a number of legends and myths were adapted to fit the new faith. The dragon, a symbol of knowledge and prosperity in Asian cultures, became a fire-breathing, horned monster that represented Satan. The vampire, a creature that lived by drinking the blood of the living and was feared throughout numerous countries, could be vanquished by the Holy Cross. The people of many ancient African cultures, including the legendary kingdom of Ethiopia, also feared restless spirits and tried to keep them at bay with the use of fetishes, small bags filled with magical objects.

As new immigrants arrived in the colonies that would eventually become the United States, they brought their beliefs with them. These supernatural tales were usually adapted to their new environment and continued to thrive as they were handed down through the generations. But long before European immigrants, carrying their belongings and beliefs, arrived in New Jersey, the Garden State was populated by the Lenni-Lenape, Native Americans who had their own tales of the paranormal. Unlike many Native Americans who were forced from their homes, some Lenni-Lenape remained in New Jersey, and their descendants have kept alive a number of traditions, including tribal legends.

When some of the first Europeans to explore and settle in what became New Jersey arrived, it is possible they thought that the Lenni-Lenape were devil worshipers. Europeans, at the time of the first contacts with New Jersey's Indians, certainly believed in witches, devil worship, ghosts, and various demons. European exploration of the New World was coming at the tail end of a period of intense witch hunts and witch burnings. It's estimated that in England alone, through the fifteenth and sixteenth centuries, thirty thousand witches had been found, tried, and sentenced to death. Thus the early settlers expected to find evidence of witchcraft and devil worship among the "heathens," and this may have shaped their first impressions. However, later arrivals, who may have gotten to know their Indian neighbors better, did not share this impression.

Three Lenni-Lenape tribes shared residency of the Garden State: the Minsi in the north, the Unami in the central portion, and the Unilachtigo in the south. The protective totems associated with each tribe were the wolf for the Minsi, the turtle for the Unami, and the turkey for the Unilachtigo. While each tribe had its own unique beliefs, they shared a number of common ones. As understood, or maybe misunderstood, by early explorers and settlers, the primary Indian religion revolved around Horitt Manitto, a Great Spirit who served as a sort of chief executive of the universe. This Great Spirit, though, seemed to function at the highest policy level only, leaving day-to-day management of his creation to Manunckus Manitto, an evil subordinate who seemed more like a devil. The Europeans immediately saw a close resemblance between Manunckus Manitto and their religious tradition of Satan as a fallen angel. The Lenape made sacrifices to their version of the devil, which took the form of "first fruits." The first fish caught on a fishing expedition was tossed into a sacrificial fire; the first deer slain on a hunting trip was similarly burned. These practices did not seem all that different from European-American traditions like tossing the first fish caught back into the sea as tribute to Neptune, god of the sea.

In addition to such sacrifices, Manunckus Manitto was placated by dances held in his honor. Interestingly, the Indians apparently believed in heaven, but not in hell. The spirits of the good people went to heaven, while the spirits of the less virtuous were in a kind of non-heaven where they could witness the pleasures of heaven but not participate in them. Sort of like forcing really poor people to watch an endless film on the lifestyles of the rich and famous.

Such varied ethnic traditions are not unique to New Jersey. Settlers throughout the American colonies handed down folktales that they had learned from their families and made them part of life in the New World. While the Garden State is not as physically large as some, it hosts an impressive number of stories about ghosts, goblins, and other things that go bump in the night. There is a geography of ghosts and hauntings. Ghosts do not appear at random but haunt special locales, even particular rooms in buildings, as many students of ghost lore have observed.

The myths and tales about the paranormal, planted so long ago by many different groups, continue to thrive from the mountain ranges of the northwest to the broad beaches of the south. We've gathered a number of these stories in an approximate geographical fashion to allow the reader a chance to enjoy some of the more colorful aspects of a region at one time. We've placed them in a general chronological order, as well, and have tried whenever possible to group the ghosts, witches, and other creatures together. When one monster tends to roam from place to place, however, we've included the story where it was first sighted. The tales begin in the north and meander south, and include everything from the cosmic to the comical and in between. Enjoy!

Northern
New Jersey

THE RUGGED HIGHLANDS OF NORTH-CENTRAL NEW JERSEY HAVE MORE than their fair share of hauntings. This land of sharp, steep ridges and narrow valleys was not especially welcoming to settlers looking for good farmland. Plowing the not-so-good soils on steep slopes was both a dangerous and unrewarding job. Indeed, until late-nineteenth-century dairies proved successful—since cows didn't mind the steep mountainsides—it was a land of few farmers.

But the real wealth of the Highlands lay not in its thin soils but in the rocks beneath, for this is iron country. The Highlands iron mines provided much of the raw material for the very bones of our civilization—iron and steel. And so it is no surprise that some of the most famous ghosts of the Highlands are the spirits of those associated with mining ores and making iron and steel.

The Ghosts of Ringwood

One place in particular seems to stand out in the haunted Highlands, and that is Ringwood Manor near the New York border. Ringwood, now a state-owned historic site, is an inviting and enjoyable visit for many New Jerseyans today. It was one of many iron-manufacturing complexes in the Highlands, but both its history and its ghosts place it high on the list of special places.

It is said that early surveyors in the Highlands, including those charged with determining the boundary there between the colonies of East Jersey and West Jersey, were convinced that the area was overrun by witches and evil spirits. Their all-important compasses clearly were bewitched, as they would spin crazily instead of pointing reliably to the north. And then there were the tales told by the local Lenni-Lenape of "magic stones"—black, heavy stones said to attract and hold smaller fragments of the same stone. Not only that, but the magic stones mysteriously attracted the Europeans' iron and steel tools and weapons.

The Europeans quickly realized that the black magic stones were magnetite iron ore—natural magnets. The race was on to find the richest veins of ore. There was magic in those stones all right—the magical ability to make some money.

There was already an iron mine at Ringwood before 1740. An interesting character (and now a ghost) entered Ringwood's history in 1764, when Peter Hasenclever, an ironmaster from Germany, arrived. A man of great charm, he had talked some wealthy investors back in London into giving him £40,000, an enormous sum at the time, to develop the mines at Ringwood. Ringwood would not only produce ore, but also smelt the ore in huge furnaces, and then forge the metal into useful forms. Hasenclever imported more than five hundred German workers to build and operate his new enterprise.

Hasenclever was a skilled ironmaster, and his products soon had a reputation as being of the highest quality. But he was even more adept at spending money than making it. He began calling himself Baron Hasenclever. His lifestyle certainly matched that of landed gentry, though there is no evidence that he had any right to such a title. The self-styled baron lived so well that his hospitality was famous, and his London backers began wondering if they would ever see a dividend. His London investors, one of whom was King George III's wife, Queen Charlotte, had a lot of influence. They insisted that the "baron" come back to London and explain himself. He returned to Ringwood in 1767 but by 1769 was disgraced and bankrupt.

Although Hasenclever is buried back in England, Ringwood—the site of both his triumph and tragedy—is said to host his ghost. Several people have seen the baron, a handsome man dressed in all the finery of an eighteenth-century aristocrat, strolling about the ponds and reservoirs that his men built at Ringwood, apparently trying to invite people to attend one of his fabulous parties.

George Washington's Geographer

Robert Erskine, an energetic mining engineer from Scotland, took over the Ringwood property in 1771. He brought the mines, all fifty-three holes, back into production and improved the furnaces and forges. Ringwood's ore production was so large that a network of roads transported the ores to other furnaces as well at Pompton, Charlotteburg, and Newfoundland.

This surge in iron production came just in time to supply vital cannons, cannonballs, and other necessities to American Revolutionaries. Many of the USS *Constitution*'s ("Old Ironsides") cannons were made at Ringwood, as were the cannonballs fired at British ships. The huge iron chain stretched across the Hudson to block British ships at West Point was, at least in part, a Ringwood product.

Erskine's iron made a big difference in the war, but his personal contributions to the war effort were even more impressive. Robert Erskine joined Gen. George Washington's staff as surveyor general and mapmaker. He produced at least two hundred detailed maps with which Washington plotted his troop positions and enemy movements. Washington's geographer died young, at the age of forty-five, and is buried in a stone crypt near Ringwood Manor. His ghost is said to have sat on top of the tomb, next to a blue lantern. It seemed that Erskine's ghost was calling attention to the deteriorating condition of his tomb, as the habit of perching on his grave ended when his descendents repaired the crypt. Robert Erskine's ghost has joined several others in roaming Ringwood Manor's nighttime hallways and rooms. It is said that his ghost also walks the grounds, checking on the ruins and buildings of what was once part of America's industrial war machine.

Other Ghosts of Ringwood

George Washington was a frequent visitor to Ringwood, and it was at Ringwood Manor that the Father of Our Country had to make an unpleasant but necessary decision to end the so-called

"Pompton Mutiny." About three hundred soldiers of Washington's army had mutinied, refusing to follow orders from their officers. Realizing that the fate of a free nation was in danger if the mutiny succeeded and spread, the general reluctantly ordered a court-martial, and two leading instigators of the mutiny were found guilty and shot. Buried without honor in unmarked graves, the ghosts of these two scoundrels wander through the woods at night. They are said to be evil, vengeful spirits, unlike the benign ghosts of Baron Hasenclever and Robert Erskine.

Other less famous ghosts of Ringwood fall into the general categories of mining or industrial deaths and military personnel. Mining iron ore and making iron were dangerous occupations. Many died in the mines or were killed in industrial accidents. The iron mines and works were so vital to the patriots' cause that the workers at Ringwood and other furnaces and forges were exempt from military service. Soldiers were brought in to protect this key industry. A group of French soldiers stationed at Ringwood suffered an epidemic of disease that sent many to an early grave and, it is said, a restless afterlife, looking for the road back to the ports where French ships awaited them. It is said that if you listen closely on almost any night, you can hear the sound of soft voices speaking French—perhaps wondering why they are still so far from home.

Ringwood Manor itself seems to be heavily populated by ghosts. Another reported supernatural resident is a housemaid who frequents the second-floor bedroom where she once slept. The young woman was reportedly beaten to death in the small room; at night, the sounds of footsteps, loud thumping noises, and soft crying supposedly can be heard echoing down the hall.

At least one local superintendent (Ringwood is now owned by the New Jersey State Park Service) has reported being visited in his office by a ghost, possibly that of Robert Erskine. The manor house is a rather awkward, rambling structure of seventy-eight rooms. To the original house of Baron Hasenclever, fine enough in its day, much larger wings were added by later owners. Supposedly other old buildings on the estate were even moved and tacked onto the sprawling structure. In the Victorian era, Gothic and Tudor trim were added, so that the manor looks like everyone's idea of a haunted house. It is reported that no one, absolutely no one, is happy about working in the manor after sundown.

The Ghost of William Franklin: A Father-and-Son Tragedy

Restored to its magnificent Colonial appearance, the governor's mansion stands near the waterfront in Perth Amboy, a rather down-at-the-heels industrial port city in northern New Jersey. In the early Colonial period, Perth Amboy served as the capital of the colony of East Jersey, while Burlington was the capital of West Jersey. When the old proprietary colonies of East and West Jersey were combined into one royal colony in 1702, Queen Anne ordered that the entire Colonial government alternate sessions between Perth Amboy and Burlington, recognizing the dual nature of New Jersey. And so Perth Amboy, along with Burlington, had a governor's mansion. It still stands. And it is haunted.

It is said that a ghost clothed in a late-eighteenth-century gentleman's costume—powdered and curled wig, velvet trousers, ornately embroidered silk waistcoat, and frilled lace shirt—roams the building at night. The troubled ghost, seen wringing its hands and lamenting over and over, "Oh, why? Why did I do it?" is that of New Jersey's last royal governor and thus the last official resident of Perth Amboy's governor's mansion. He carried a famous name, William Franklin, but he carried it into infamy in contrast to his illustrious father, Benjamin.

Ben Franklin—philosopher, scientist, diplomat and statesman, author and businessman, patriot—was a most practical man. Born poor but ambitious, Ben had an eye for ladies, fame, and fortune, not necessarily in that order. He appreciated money, though he did not worship it. He got himself appointed colonial postmaster and pulled all the strings he could to get his only son, William, appointed royal governor of New Jersey. It was a prestigious and well-paid post. Gov. William Franklin reported directly to the king, to whom he had sworn loyalty. William was fairly popular and successful as governor, at least up until the Revolution. Then William made a very serious mistake—one he came to regret for the rest of his life and, indeed, continues to regret as a ghost.

William decided to stick with his pledge of loyalty to His British Majesty, King George III. His father, Ben, was an ardent American patriot who did his best to persuade William to support the Revolutionary cause and disavow his loyalty to the king. William had a chance to declare his American patriotism and, very likely, be recognized as an American patriot, rather than British royal, governor. But to Ben's great regret and shame, William stayed loyal to the Crown and was placed under house arrest in his opulent governor's mansion. He stubbornly refused to join the Revolution, though he was given repeated chances to change sides. In William's view, he refused to betray his king's trust. In Ben's view, his son betrayed his country, his countrymen, and his own father.

How different it might have been! If William had followed his father's lead, he could have been in the top ranks of American leaders of the Revolution. Ben's influence and contacts would have opened many opportunities for William as an American patriot. But William died alone and forgotten in England—an exile from home, without family or friends. No wonder that, overwhelmed by guilt, regret, and shame, William's ghost still wanders the governor's mansion, his last American home, expressing his remorse.

Ben Franklin could never forgive his only son's breaking of God's commandment to honor one's father and mother. The story is told that when a ship carrying Ben home from a diplomatic mission to France anchored off the coast of England, Ben refused to go ashore to visit with his son, then in exile. Mutual friends persuaded William to go out to the ship in a rowboat for one last meeting with his still angry father. Ben, it turned out, had only agreed to see William so that he could present his son with a bill for having raised him, only to see his son support the enemy. William didn't pay in cash, but he paid over and over again in inner turmoil and self-hatred. No wonder William Franklin's restless ghost still expresses his profound but too-late regrets: "Oh, why? Why did I do it? Why did I turn my back on my father and my country?"

Captain Huddy's Ghost

It is said that many have seen a man, clad in the uniform of a Revolutionary War officer, wandering along the shores of Sandy Hook. The apparition seems intent on approaching the observer, and then at the last moment turns away and mysteriously disappears. This disappearing act usually occurs just after the soldier has heard the voices of those he met. Was he listening for an English accent?

Woe to the Englishman that the officer meets on his lonely patrols, for many believe that the lonely figure is the ghost of Capt. Joshua Huddy, who still prowls the beaches, seeking vengeance on the British troops who hanged him for murder—a murder they knew he did not commit.

Capt. Joshua Huddy, from a prominent Monmouth County family, was hanged from a tall tree atop the Highlands on April 12, 1782. Surely his last sight on earth was of Sandy Hook and Sandy Hook Bay, where he had valiantly served his country, only to be foully murdered by his opponents, the British army of occupation.

Sandy Hook in those days was of great importance to both the Americans and the British. The Revolutionaries needed to watch British ship movements to and from New York City, which was occupied by the enemy. The British needed to protect Sandy Hook Lighthouse against the rebels trying to destroy it in order to increase the chances of British shipwrecks. British naval squadrons frequently assembled in the shelter of Sandy Hook Bay and topped off their casks of fresh water at the "spout," a clear, cool spring at the foot of the Highlands, which had been visited by sailors since the days of Henry Hudson.

In the course of leading an attack on British troops stationed on Sandy Hook, Captain Huddy was captured. His captors, continually harassed by American patrols and very much aware of being observed by American spies, were lusting to find an excuse, any excuse, to make an example of a rebel. They accused Captain Huddy of having killed Philip White, a British soldier. It was a trumped-up charge, and the British knew it could not be true. Philip White had been shot after Captain Huddy had been taken prisoner. But hang him they did, and in doing so created a martyr to the American cause.

The public on both sides of the Atlantic was outraged when the treachery and vindictiveness of the British commanders became known. But more than a martyr was created on that April day so long ago. The restless spirit of the wronged soldier still roams the bayshores, watching for British warships approaching and making sure that any people encountered on his nightly patrols are true and patriotic Americans.

The Tale of Jennie McRea

Jennie McRea was the daughter of a New Jersey clergyman who, like Shakespeare's Juliet, fell in love with the wrong man at the wrong place and time. Her lover was an American colonist who chose to fight for the British during the Revolutionary War. As a result, Jennie's angered father forbade her to ever again see the man he considered a traitor.

Like many young women in love, Jennie didn't care about politics and only wanted to be with the man she loved. Determined to join him, even if it meant permanent banishment from her family and her country, she packed her bags and began traveling north toward New York State, where he was stationed with British troops.

Some say that Jenny hired two Indians, who worked for the British, to lead her to her lover's camp. Others say that she was abducted by some Indians, again in the enemy's employ, while on her journey. In either event, a group of American soldiers reportedly came along and, upon seeing Jennie with the Indians, opened fire. In the scuffle that followed, she was shot and killed.

The Indians, undoubtedly hoping to reap some reward—whether for killing an American or just to prove that she had been with them—scalped the young woman before fleeing. They brought the mass of dark curls to the British camp, where Jennie's distraught lover realized the significance of what they carried. It was said that the heartbroken young man carried the scalp beneath his coat into battle, where he repeatedly rushed into the heart of the fighting. To his dismay, he never suffered more than a few slight injuries.

Resigning his commission, the young man retired from public view. Jennie's spirit apparently haunted her lover for the rest of his life. He annually marked the day of her passing in silent meditation in a locked room. To this day, no one knows what happened to the remains of the young woman who was willing to sacrifice everything for love.

The Hollow Earth Theory

Most people would find it hard to believe, but the very first journey to the center of the earth actually began in New Jersey. Not at a particular location. Rather, in the mind of John Cleves Symmes, who was born in the Garden State around 1779. Contrary to those who turned their gaze to the heavens at that time, Symmes cast his eyes down to the ground, believing that the earth was hollow and that it sustained life underneath the surface.

Symmes was the nephew and namesake of a prominent New Jersey Superior Court judge, who was well known in state and federal political circles. A soldier who served as a captain during the War of 1812, Symmes later retired from the army to pursue philosophical studies. He focused especially on ancient texts that speculated about another world beneath ours. In 1818, he sparked a worldwide furor with his theory that the earth was composed of six or seven concentric hollow spheres, which were accessible at points located at both the North and South Poles.

Symmes lectured nationwide and eventually approached the U.S. Congress about funding an expedition that would allow him to prove his theories. According to the *Journal of the Senate of the United States of America, 1789–1873*, on Thursday, March 7, 1822, Kentucky representative Johnson presented a petition drafted by the former soldier, "stating his belief of the existence of an inhabited concave to this globe; his desire to embark on a voyage of discovery to one or other of the polar regions; [and] his belief in the value and honor to his country of the discoveries which he would make." Citing insufficient personal funds, Symmes asked that Congress equip two vessels for him along with "such other aid as the government may deem requisite to promote the object" of his quest. Upon a motion by Tennessee representative Williams, his petition was duly tabled and ultimately forgotten by government officials after the session adjourned.

Although his detractors ridiculed him, Symmes continued to publish his arguments in prominent publications such as the *Atlantic Monthly*. He eventually inspired many fiction writers to create tales about life under the surface of the earth, including noted American author Edgar Allan Poe, who captured Symmes's ideas in the science-fiction tale *The Narrative of Arthur Gordon Pym*. Jules Verne's popular *Journey to the Center of the Earth* was another tale that speculated about traveling beneath the earth's crust. Over the years, the concept was periodically revived by authors such as Marshall B. Gardner, who wrote *A Journey to the Earth's Interior*. Gardner's 1913 book described a subterranean world that included an interior sun, six hundred miles in diameter, which created a tropical environment for the inhabitants of that world. Less than twenty years later, H. Spencer Lewis authored *The Lost Continent of the Pacific*. This was yet another tale based on Symmes's theories, but this time, Lewis added the remains of a super-race that lived inside Mount Shasta in northern California. Most recently, the idea became the basis of a science-fiction movie titled *The Core*.

During the nineteenth century, a number of free thinkers avidly studied Symmes' theories. These included his son, Americus Vespucius, and H. P. Blavatsky, the founder of the Theosophists School, a group devoted to the study of the occult. In the late nineteenth century, Cyrus Teed developed the concept of Koreshanity, a religion based on Symmes's theories. The followers of Koreshanity apparently believed that the universe was a hollow globe, in which revolved the sun, moon, earth, and other planets.

Most people either ignored or ridiculed the ex-soldier's ideas, however. With little public support and no financial backing from the government for an expedition to prove his arguments, Symmes eventually faded from public view and moved to Ohio, where he died at age forty-nine in May 1829. In the 1840s, Americus erected a memorial to his father in the city of Hamilton, Ohio, which features a hollow globe on top of a four-sided column. It still stands today behind a cast-iron fence and is inscribed with a record of Symmes's bravery as a soldier. The New Jersey native is described as "a philosopher, and the originator of Symmes Theory of Concentric Spheres and Polar Voids; He contended that the Earth is hollow and habitable within."

Cruel and Unusual Punishment

The restless spirit of Antoine LeBlanc haunts Morristown, where he was hanged in the early nineteenth century for the horrific crime of multiple murder. Legend has it that LeBlanc wants his body parts returned to one resting place.

The grisly tale began in April 1833, when LeBlanc, a French immigrant, was offered the position of gardener for a wealthy Morristown resident named Samuel Sayre. After accepting the job, LeBlanc resided with the family for barely one week before he murdered Sayre and his wife, and their servant, Phoebe.

The murders both scandalized and intrigued the nation. While there were no supermarket tabloids like the *National Enquirer* in those days, speedily published brochures known as "penny dreadfuls" appeared whenever such crimes were committed. The story was recorded in one titled *Murder of the Sayre Family at Morristown, New Jersey, by Antoine LeBlanc, May 11, 1833,* written less than a month after the murders occurred. In the pamphlet, LeBlanc confessed to killing the Sayres and their servant because "my object only was money." Greed apparently got the better of him, as he stuffed pillowcases full of the family's property before climbing on his horse.

His life of crime was a short one, because LeBlanc was not a skilled criminal. Authorities soon captured him after following a trail of the Sayres' stolen goods to his door. Apparently, unknown to LeBlanc, they had fallen from the back of his horse when he fled the scene of his heinous crime.

LeBlanc was ultimately tried and hanged for his crimes, and his body was turned over to a local surgeon, Dr. Isaac Canfield, for dissection. At a time when medicine was still a fledgling science, such opportunities allowed doctors a chance to study internal organs, skeletal structure, and other aspects of physical development. It appears, however, that Dr. Canfield did more than study LeBlanc's body. After various experiments were performed on the corpse, the criminal's skin was tanned and used to make pocketbooks and other mementos. According to Henry C. Beck in *The Roads of Home,* "The ghost of this villain is said to come back over the ground of his last earthly journey every now and then, looking for a gruesome pocketbook." One such purse remains in existence today in the possession of the New Jersey Historical Society, headquartered in Newark.

New Jersey's Royal Ghost

On the north side of Bordentown is a housing development known as Point Breeze, where some residents report strange noises—sounds of footsteps coming from beneath their feet, underground, and the faint sounds of partying: conversations just too low to be understood, laughter, clinking glasses, and faint music. On occasion, in deep winter, a mysterious figure appears to watch ice skaters on a local pond. The figure rolls oranges and apples out onto the ice toward the skaters. But as the skaters chase these gifts, the fruit disappears.

Is the dark spectator of the ice skaters the ghost of the one-time king of Spain and former king of Naples? By all accounts, Joseph Bonaparte, older brother of Napoleon Bonaparte, was a kind and generous, if somewhat aloof, neighbor of Bordentown residents in the early nineteenth century. His fortunes rose and fell with his more famous brother's victories and defeats. Forced to abandon his throne when Napoleon's armies retreated, Joseph sought refuge in the New World. When Pennsylvania would not allow an alien to buy land (Bonaparte refused to apply for American citizenship), New Jersey passed a special act enabling the former king to buy eighteen hundred acres at Point Breeze.

Joseph Bonaparte explained that Napoleon had once said that if he were forced into exile, he would choose America, where British demands for extradition would not be honored. Napoleon is supposed to have placed his finger on a huge world globe, at a point precisely halfway between New York and Philadelphia, as the prime location for exile, easily accessible to these two great ports to learn the latest news from France.

Bonaparte built a mansion and began to entertain the important political and social figures of his day. The Marquis de Lafayette, John Adams, John Clay, and Daniel Webster all enjoyed the hospitality at Point Breeze. Calling himself the Count de Survilliers, Bonaparte allowed his neighbors to use the park he had created from wilderness and encouraged them to ice skate on his pond in winter. It was Bonaparte's habit of rolling oranges and apples out on the ice for his visitors to chase that seems to be perpetuated by his ghost. The Point Breeze estate had secret tunnels connecting the house to the riverbank and to a road, as Bonaparte feared that English or Spanish agents might try to assassinate him or kidnap him.

When the first house burned down, Bonaparte's neighbors helped him bring out valuable furniture and paintings. When a bedroom chest, loaded with gold coins, was retrieved and returned to the former king intact, he was both grateful and astonished. In France, he noted, under those circumstances, the coins and the furniture both would have been looted.

Joseph Bonaparte really liked Americans, and his neighbors liked his generosity and the glamour of his social life. Bonaparte had a carefree life here, out from under the shadow of his famous younger brother. Although he returned to Europe as an old man, dying in Florence in 1844, his ghost may have preferred to return to the scene of his happiest days. Bonaparte's wife, an unpleasant woman, refused to come to America with him, and Joseph had a series of lovely young mistresses while at Point Breeze—another reason to lure his ghost back to New Jersey!

Neighborhood Feud

Don't mention the name of John Field in the Metlar-Bodine House in Piscataway. Although more than a hundred years have passed, it seems that the ghost of George Metlar grows extremely agitated whenever Field's name is brought up in conversation. Metlar was a wealthy land baron from New Brunswick who, like many rich men of the period, dabbled in various enterprises. He was the last private owner of the fourteen-room mansion located on the Raritan Landing, first constructed by Peter Bodine in 1728.

Although no one knows how the feud started, Metlar apparently never forgave Field, his next-door neighbor, for some real or imagined slight. His anger seems to have carried over into the next world: Visitors to the mansion have reported cold spots and strange noises at different points throughout the house whenever Field's name is mentioned. Once a picture of Field was discovered facedown on a fireplace hearth.

In 1977, the property was purchased by the state of New Jersey, and the house was slated for demolition. However, local residents persuaded the Department of Transportation that it should be preserved because of its historic significance. Today the property is maintained by the township of Piscataway and the Fellowship for Metlar House, a nonprofit organization.

From the Ramapo Mountains

Like the residents of many insular communities, the folks who live in the Ramapo Mountains have developed a rich folklore about their region, revolving around everything from physical features to the inhabitants. One story describes how at least part of the region's rough terrain developed when an apparently domesticated Devil was traveling through the region carrying a big pile of rocks in his apron, much like a homemaker carrying vegetables from the garden. Something happened, and before Old Nick knew it, a large pile of rocks fell from his apron to the ground. The place, filled with rocky formations, is familiar to many mountain residents, and, according to David Cohen in *The Rampo Mountain People,* is simply referred to as "where the devil broke his apron strings."

As snakes are a real and constant danger in their region, the local residents also have developed a number of tall reptile tales over the years. The "joint snake" is said to rest in pieces until it spots a person passing by. Then the pieces join together and slither after him down the road. The "hoop snake" will grab his tail in his mouth and roll down the roadside behind unsuspecting passers-by. If they stop, however, the snake will drop his tail and slither off, until they start moving again. Then the snake will crawl out of the bushes, grab his tail, and roll down the road again. The "crown snake" is also known as the "king of snakes" because it wears a real crown. However, once the snake throws its crown at a person, it retreats and dies.

The White Pilgrim

They called him the "White Pilgrim"—the wandering preacher from Ohio who dressed entirely in white clothing. Joseph Thomas was an Ohio native born about 1790, who first visited New Jersey around 1835. At a time when most working-class people wore drab, homespun clothes, he cut an impressive figure in all white clothing, including white hat and boots. Thomas also rode a white horse as he traveled from town to town. He believed that the color white, a symbol of purity, not only warded off evil, but also protected him from the epidemics that ran rampant at the time.

Shortly after his arrival, he was invited to preach at Johnson-burg's Episcopal Church. Ironically, Thomas was struck down by smallpox not long after finishing his sermon. Fear of contagion caused local residents to first inter his body at a small, private cemetery behind the Dark of the Moon, a notorious tavern where anything could—and frequently did—happen. The White Pilgrim's body was later moved to the town's public cemetery, but the obelisk that marks his grave is located at a distance from his neighbors, as though to prevent the spread of disease even after death. Some say that on moonless nights, Thomas's ghost can be seen hovering around the cemetery of the Episcopal Church at Johnsonburg, as though still determined to preach to the local population.

Water-Dwelling Monsters

Water-dwelling monsters hold an especially terrifying fascination because we can't see them, at least not until it is clearly too late. What we can't see, we can't understand. And what we don't understand, we fear. Since the early Colonial period, people have reported strange creatures dwelling variously in the Delaware River, the Atlantic Ocean off the New Jersey coast, and Lake Hopatcong.

Early settlers told of a mysterious monster dwelling in Lake Hopatcong. It was described rather vaguely as having the head of a horse, a moose, or a large deer—the stories vary. It occasionally upset boats on the lake, frightening but not otherwise harming the fishermen who get dunked unexpectedly. One early theory was that the monster of the lake was a deer or moose that had taken to a wholly aquatic life, having located a good source of food and an environment safe from predators.

Other versions of the Lake Hopatcong sightings describe a more serpentlike creature, with an elongated neck and an undulating swimming motion more characteristic of snakes. This sounds a little more like the descriptions of that more famous lake monster that makes its home in Scotland's Loch Ness.

The Swedes who pioneered in the Delaware Valley during the seventeenth century saw at least two different river monsters. It is said that the local Indians called these beasts Manitto, or devil-fish. One type was described as a headless, boneless mass of jellylike or spongy substance. It could project its bowels outward quickly to envelop a fish, surrounding its prey and then sucking it into its shapeless body. A second type was a more serpentlike monster with the head of a dog. This one could sever a man's leg in one bite. It could allegedly swim much faster than a man and could hurl itself ashore to catch an unwary fisherman on the banks.

Brant, the Indian Chief

There is an old story told in Wantage, up in Sussex County, about the miraculous escape of some innocent young schoolgirls from an Indian massacre in July 1781. A band of Indians, outraged by the land-grabbing of their white neighbors, decided on a preemptive strike. Their ancestral hunting grounds were being fenced off by the European settlers, who seemed limitless in number. The chief, known as Brant, had about the same reputation among the whites as a lion would have among gazelles. Brant was much feared as a clever, ruthless leader who had no love whatsoever for the English-Americans then intruding on Indian lands.

Brant supposedly inflamed the hearts of his warriors with a determination to drive out the whites through a reign of terror, killing every one they found. And so a band of warriors descended on a one-room school recently established by the local farmers to educate their children. The schoolmaster was killed first and dragged out to the road as an example to other settlers. A few of the older boys tried to protect their teacher and were quickly dispatched by tomahawks. The girls fled into the woods until the Indians had departed, and then gathered by the corpse of the schoolmaster to cry and comfort one another.

At this point, the much-feared and ruthless chief, Brant happened by. Even Brant was horrified by what he saw—a defenseless schoolteacher beaten to death by war axes, and a group of young girls huddled next to his bloody body, terrified out of their minds. How could this be an honorable war? Brant did his best to calm the girls. Using black paint, he painted a magical sign on their white aprons, telling them that any warrior, on seeing this sign, would leave them alone. And the sign worked. The girls were left alone.

Today, Brant's ghost roams the mountains, wearing that same magical sign of good luck. It was a common symbol among American Indians and always had a positive meaning. It was the German Nazis of the twentieth century who gave the swastika a sinister meaning.

Tom Quick and the Ninety-nine Indian Ghosts

The French and Indian Wars (1756–63) produced one of New Jersey's most famous Indian fighters, Tom Quick. As the story goes, he killed ninety-nine Indians in his thirst for revenge after they killed his family. It is said that his only regret was that he hadn't rounded off his kills with a hundredth victim. Despite his bloodthirsty behavior, he was said to be deathly afraid of the ghosts of his victims.

Fought primarily between the British and the French, the French and Indian Wars were a series of basically indecisive battles between the two mighty empires, contesting control of most of North America. The French had persuaded many Indians that their best interests lay in stopping the rapid expansion of Britain's Atlantic Seaboard colonies, so the British found themselves also fighting different tribes throughout the territory.

Tom Quick had been a peaceable enough man until 1757, the second year of the French and Indian Wars. Tom's father had emigrated from Holland in the 1730s. One of the early pioneers in the Upper Delaware Valley, he had built a sawmill and a gristmill on the Pennsylvania side of the river above the Delaware Water Gap. His mills, on a small tributary of the Delaware, prospered. The Quick family earned a reputation for fair dealing, not only among Dutch and English settlers, but among the local Indians as well. Tom, it is claimed, grew up among Indians who lived close by, learning several Indian dialects, and hunting and fishing with Indian boys as though they were cousins.

But the local Indians, treated well enough by the Quick family, had a general grudge against the white invaders who had taken their ancestral lands. The Indians knew that they'd been swindled out of land by the untrustworthy Europeans. The Pennsylvania side of the Upper Delaware was the location of the notorious "walking purchase." The deal was that the British were to buy a tract of land on the west bank of the Upper Delaware for a fixed sum. This land would extend as far as a man could walk in one day, sunup to sundown. Through rough terrain, this would amount typically to about thirty or forty miles, tops. But the unscrupulous English hired athletes, who were given orders not to stop for anything. These

marathon runners ran eighty-six miles in one day, to the angry astonishment of the Indians.

At first, as the French and Indian Wars began, the Quicks felt safe in their friendship with the Indians. Then Tom's family was ambushed. During the fighting, his father fell, mortally wounded, and told Tom to save himself and get revenge. Tom could hear his father's screams as he fled, because the attackers brutally scalped his father alive. Not long afterward, Tom began his lifelong campaign of revenge, at first killing only warriors, but later wiping out whole families. He became a bloodthirsty character who liked to be known as the "Avenger of the Delaware."

At one point, Tom entered a local tavern on the Jersey side of the river where he spent most of his time. He recognized a boyhood friend, an Indian called Muskwink, who invited him to share a drink of rum. Tom had a drink or two, and then recognized the silver buttons on Muskwink's coat as having belonged to his father. Muskwink, by now drunk, admitted to the killing, boasting that he made the old man suffer before death. Tom marched Muskwink out the door and beat him to death in front of an approving mob. Tom was on his way to becoming a local hero, continuing the killing even after peace was declared. An expert marksman, he went right on shooting any Indian he came across.

Tom knew that Indian traditions supported a belief in ghosts, and he believed in ghosts, too. When Tom killed an Indian, he buried the corpse in a shallow grave, facedown as a further insult, so the person would never again see sun, moon, or stars. It is said that Tom returned periodically to scatter the bones, hoping to destroy the ghosts of the deceased. But as Tom learned, such desecration of the graves simply angered the ghosts all the more. He was eventually haunted by ninety-nine ghosts.

Although the colonial government of New Jersey was not exactly a friend of the Indians, there was real fear that Tom would start another Indian war all by himself. As the story goes, Tom was captured by soldiers who were to transport him to Newton to stand trial. On their way, with Tom securely tied up in the back of a wagon, the soldiers stopped for a drink at a tavern—the same one where Tom had killed his father's murderer.

While a local fiddler "fiddled up a storm" to help distract the soldiers, who were having a few rum toddies, Tom's neighbors freed him and sent him on his way. Tom supposedly hid out on a small, deserted island in the Delaware River, and friends rowed supplies out to him on moonless nights. Tom lived for years on this little island, visited every night by ninety-nine ghosts.

Tom Quick eventually died in bed, a victim of smallpox. When the local Indians learned of his death, they decided to dig up his body and offer it to the vultures as prey, a final insult to their great enemy. But old Tom had the last, bitter laugh, as it is claimed that several more Indians died of the smallpox they contracted from the corpse. Tom finally got his wish of topping a hundred Indian souls in vengeance for the death of his father.

The ninety-nine Indian ghosts still roam the steep ridges and narrow valleys of northwestern New Jersey, and chasing after them, as in life, is the troubled ghost of Tom Quick—as locals joke, "The Quick and the dead."

The Great Chief Who Wouldn't Leave His People

In the Highlands around New Jersey's Lake Hopatcong, they tell the story of a great chief who wouldn't leave his people, even in death.

It seems that Quaquahela, a great sachem, or chief, who was much admired and trusted by his people, decided to go off on his own for a while, a kind of vacation from the pressures of leadership. He would be gone, he announced, for thirteen moons, or about a year. When his people objected to his leaving them leaderless, Quaquahela replied that others must step up to leadership responsibilities until he came back.

No sooner had Quaquahela left the village when a terrible uproar began in the deep woods. An enraged bear was bellowing and growling. Later that day, some braves found a huge bear that had bled to death because of fatal wounds, which apparently had been inflicted by Chief Quaquahela. The chief's war club and bow and arrows were found nearby, drenched in blood. But what had happened to the great and respected sachem?

That night, a warrior dreamed that the chief had visited him with an important message. Quaquahela was deeply ashamed of himself. He had selfishly abandoned his people, and the Great Spirit had punished him for that. A great bear had been sent to attack him, knowing that Quaquahela must defend himself. In a life-and-death struggle, the chief had overcome the bear but had been mortally wounded himself. A bear had been Quaquahela's own totem, his personal symbol, and so it was a sacrilegious act to kill one, even in self-defense. The sachem's spirit could not rest peacefully after that.

But Quaquahela could redeem himself by staying with his people always. As foretold in the warrior's dream, Quaquahela appeared as a pillar of smoke. Whenever an important decision had to be made by the tribe, the pillar of smoke would lead the way to a solution. If the Indians were beset by enemies, the pillar of smoke would lead them to reliable allies. If they lacked food, the pillar of smoke would lead them to abundant game.

It is said that the pillar of smoke still appears to Indians in trouble around the shores of Lake Hopatcong.

Newark's Gully Road Ghost

A great many ghost stories tell of haunted houses or other haunted buildings. But what happens when the house occupied in life is no longer standing? What's a poor ghost to do?

As frequently is the case, Newark's Gully Road ghost has a grievance. The story goes that an aged couple lived in a little house, which they'd built themselves, on the edge of Newark—a city that was growing rapidly in the late nineteenth century. Their house was next to a small brook. The brook dried up, perhaps because new arrivals in the neighborhood were digging wells nearby, and people began using the now-dry bed as a convenient roadway. Traffic got heavier, and the road needed to be widened. The old couple was ordered to abandon their house. They refused.

During the tension and harassment that followed, the wife died of stress. Her grieving husband, more determined than ever to stay, had to leave when his house was demolished over his head. He, too, died—according to friends, of a broken and bitter heart.

His ghost now wanders along the highway that gave him so much grief. Many a late-night motorist has seen a man, bent with age, suddenly dart into the traffic lane, causing them to brake hard and swerve. But if their vehicle doesn't avoid the seemingly unaware pedestrian, there is no collision. The man simply disappears, leaving a badly shaken driver.

Although his main purpose seems to be to slow down traffic near his former home, the Gully Road ghost once appeared to teach a disobedient wife a lesson. A neighborhood couple had had an argument. The elderly husband was anxious that his wife stay home. He was afraid that in her absence, he might suffer a "spell" and die alone. His wife, determined to go out anyway, drove off in the car. As she turned onto the old Gully Road, a figure jumped out in front of her, holding up his hands to bring her to a halt. She stopped, but then no one was there. Badly frightened, she returned home in time to comfort her dying husband.

Newark's Witch, Moll DeGrow

In the early nineteenth century, Newark had a resident witch, whose name was Moll DeGrow. Her evil reputation was used to scare kids into staying home on dark nights. Whatever went wrong in town was blamed on Moll. Did the milk go sour? Did the cuddly puppy suddenly turn vicious? Did a glass of wine suddenly shatter? It must be that old witch, Moll! The pranks gradually took a more serious turn. Healthy babies died without cause. Horses bolted away at midnight, never to be seen again. Something had to be done about Moll. Finally a local mob approached her little shack, carrying firebrands with which to burn the witch.

But when the mob reached her modest dwelling, they discovered her already dead in her chair. Ever since, any open flame in that vicinity is suddenly and mysteriously extinguished. Candles go out, hearth fires die. Moll is apparently still about—at least in spirit—and she doesn't like fire!

The Story of John Thompson

John Thompson was a seafaring man who called Newark his home. John worked on boats out of the port of Newark. He was known as a hard-working, hard-drinking, hard-swearing man. His vocabulary of curses was unsurpassed. John Thompson was an artist in words of damnation, a man who stood out even among sailors, a group known for foul mouths, especially after an evening of heavy drinking.

Late one moonless night, John was walking home with an ine-briated companion. Having shared way too many drinks, they were stumbling along a dark street having a swearing contest. Each was creating long, colorful strings of curses, one more obscenely rich in condemnation than the other.

Gradually the realization seeped into their drunken minds that they were not alone. A third man, a stranger, had joined them. The stranger laughed uproariously at their foul language, slapping them on their backs and encouraging yet more outrageous cursing. The man was dressed like a parson, in simple black and white.

But, John suddenly wondered, why would a parson be so delighted in the swearing? It was then that John Thompson, king of cursing, glanced down at the feet of the "parson." His feet were cloven hooves. Scared silent, John and his sailor companion ran all the way home. It is even claimed that they swore off drinking.

The Treasure of Schooley's Mountain

Legendary showman P. T. Barnum used to say of the customers who flocked to his sideshows, "There's a sucker born every minute." However, Barnum wasn't the first to realize that some people will believe anything and will pay accordingly. According to noted New Jersey author Frank Stockton, Schooley's Mountain was the site of one eighteenth-century con game that involved not only pirates and buried treasure, but evil spirits as well.

Schooley's Mountain, once known as Schugl's Hills and later Schooler's Mountain, is part of the rugged chain that extends across New Jersey's northwest corner. Still in existence, the town of the same name is located near Morristown, about fifty miles southwest of New York. At one time, it was remarkable for the mineral springs that are located near the top of the six-hundred-foot mountain. Schooley's, named for the family that once owned most of the mountain, eventually became the site of a health spa where the wealthy went to "take the waters." Remarkable cures have been attributed to the springs. But something even more remarkable allegedly occurred there during the Colonial period.

The year was 1788. Some local residents had learned about a fortune in pirate's loot that was supposedly buried up on the moun-tain. But the gold and jewels were said to be guarded by the ghosts of wicked pirates, who were no less dangerous in death than they had been life. The town notables gathered together to discuss the problem and finally decided there was only one way they could safely acquire the treasure: Someone had to get rid of the ghosts.

As a result, they decided to hire Ransford Rogers, a schoolteacher from Connecticut who claimed he could reason with the spirits and persuade them to leave—for a small fee, of course. Rogers was tired of teaching, which didn't pay very well, and shrewdly realized that the residents were offering him an opportunity that was too good to pass up.

By all accounts, Rogers was an intelligent man who enjoyed experimenting with chemistry. After he arrived in town, Rogers used his talents to arrange a display of fireworks that fooled the townspeople into believing that evil spirits, in fact, were present on the mountain. Then, using "automatic writing," a means of communication by which spirits supposedly guide the writer's hand, he persuaded the men that they must each pay him 12 pounds in gold or silver before they would be led to the treasure. Trusting their new friend, and hungry to obtain the buried loot, the men gladly paid, reasoning that it was money well spent. Twelve pounds times forty men equaled 480 pounds, about $1,200 today, a small fortune in those times.

However, Rogers apparently became a little too greedy. The unscrupulous schoolmaster tried to con the locals a second time before he would agree to dispose of the ghosts, but word of his activities reached local authorities. It seems that the local grocer found it difficult to gather the additional 12 pounds. When his wife discovered him searching their house for the money, the grocer broke down and admitted why he needed it.

Shocked and angered, the woman ran to the sheriff, who was soon on Rogers's trail. The schoolteacher was quickly arrested but just as quickly escaped from custody and, by all accounts, was last seen galloping away over the mountainside. He allegedly left New Jersey, and the local residents never saw him—or their money—again. However, it is possible that the ghosts of the pirates who guarded the treasure resented his efforts to deceive the locals, and that both Rogers's body and the money lie with the rest of the gold that, to this day, is said to be buried within Schooley's Mountain.

The Haunted Library

Historic Bernardsville, once known as Vealtown, is home to one of the oldest buildings in Somerset County, a structure that today is part of the Bernardsville Public Library. The library offers visitors more than books, research materials, and compact disks. If you're there at just the right moment, on just the right night, you might catch a glimpse of the resident ghost, a young woman named Phyllis Parker.

Phyllis's tragic story began in 1777, when the building that is now the library was the Vealtown Tavern and Inn, a popular resting place for American troops fighting in the Revolutionary War. The tavern offered weary soldiers a chance to eat and sleep as they traveled between the town of Pluckemin and Gen. George Washington's headquarters in Morristown.

The daughter of Capt. John Parker, the tavern owner, seventeen-year-old Phyllis was an attractive, dark-haired young woman who assisted her father in operating his establishment. One fateful day, a young physician named Dr. Byram decided to rent rooms at the inn, and before long, he and Phyllis were in love. But the couple was not destined to share a happy life together.

During an overnight stay at the inn, Gen. Anthony Wayne discovered that some top-secret military documents had been stolen from his rooms. While questioning the Parkers, Wayne saw a picture of the young doctor in Phyllis's room. The general immediately recognized Byram as a British spy and sent out troops in search of him. The doctor, who had disappeared shortly after the documents were discovered missing, was captured after he arrived at the nearby town of Blazure's Corner. He was given a speedy trial and hanged as a spy.

According to Valerie Barnes Cavnar in *The Strange and Mysterious Past in the Somerset Hills Area*, "Dr. Byram's last request was to write a letter to the Parkers asking them to give his body a decent burial." After the hanging, Byram's body was transported back to the tavern.

Although Phyllis's father had tried to keep the hanging victim's identity a secret, she snuck downstairs late one night after overhearing some soldiers talking about the incident. Stepping into the darkened back room, she raised the candle she carried and was shocked to see a coffin hidden there. With a shaking hand, she lifted the lid and saw Byram's body lying within. Her anguished scream echoed throughout the tavern, and shortly afterward, Phyllis went insane with grief. She died shortly thereafter and, by all accounts, haunts her family home to this day.

Although for many years, reports of spectral activity were limited, it seemed that none of the owners who came afterward felt comfortable living at the inn for any length of time. The most impressive demonstration of Phyllis's presence occurred one hundred years later, on the anniversary of her heartbreaking discovery. That night, the owners of the building reported hearing the tromping of soldiers' feet, the sound of splintering wood, and the frightful wailing of a woman. They moved not long afterward.

Her presence apparently remained after the building became Bernardsville's public library in the early 1900s. *Phyllis: The Library Ghost,* compiled by Eileen Luz Johnston, includes the recent tale of a young boy who was visiting the library and called his mother to the library's reading room to "come look at the lady" who was wearing a floor-length dress and standing by the fireplace. When the mother walked in, she discovered her son was pointing to nothing at all. What the woman did not know was that it was at that exact spot, when the reading room was the former storage room, where Phyllis had discovered Byram's remains.

Many staff members swear that a presence accompanied them while setting up a new wing in the library a few years ago. Computer equipment was mysteriously unplugged and programs were tampered with, all when staff was absent from the room. For a while, it was difficult to persuade anyone to work nights, but this situation changed as Phyllis made fewer and fewer appearances.

Will Phyllis appear again? In the event that she does return, in an effort to make the restless spirit feel more at home, the librarians issued Phyllis her own library card. She hasn't used it. After all, closing time doesn't apply to her.

The Switchback Canal

A number of legends have been documented that are associated with the "Switchback Canal," a nickname for the Morris Canal, which operated for some 150 years. On December 31, 1824, a company called the Morris Canal and Banking Company was incorporated to create a canal between the Passaic and Delaware Rivers. This was not an easy canal to build, as its route lay at right angles to New Jersey's northeast-southwest-trending mountains and valleys. The canal was a desperate attempt to help keep industry alive in New Jersey, since many iron furnaces and glass companies were beginning to move to the Midwest, where cheaper fuel sources were available. However, there was apparently more than iron and glass goods moving along the canal. According to Henry C. Beck in *The Roads of Home:* "The canal . . . had its ghosts and men of mystery. There was the boatman who was reputed to be forever wandering up and down the towpath in search of his lost wife. He had committed suicide, you see, on her running off with another boatman." The Morris Canal has since been drained and abandoned and today is a ghost of a canal.

Another story about the Morris Canal relates how the crew of the *Lager Bier* robbed and murdered a gambler from Paterson who had sought sanctuary on their boat. The unfortunate man should have considered that the word *bier* is German for the platform beneath a coffin before he made his choice, but the gambler was more afraid of the losers in the card game he had won, fearing that they would track him down if he traveled by horse or train in order to get back their gold.

It wasn't long after he boarded the canal boat that the captain and his mate discovered what he was carrying and killed the gambler without hesitation. In an effort to escape discovery, they buried the gold and the gambler along the canal banks, but no one ever returned to claim the treasure. In the years that followed, the riverbanks were repeatedly searched, but no one could find the treasure.

Although no one has ever reported seeing the gambler's ghost, another spirit is said to haunt the banks of the canal searching for the buried loot. One of the canal company's towpath walkers, "Old Man" Crane, was reportedly obsessed with the tale and searched for the gold as he walked the banks performing his job—watching for leaks, weeding the tall grass, and destroying muskrats. Crane was reportedly discovered one day lying dead by a big oak tree that he apparently suspected was a place where the treasure was buried. Did he finally get too close? Did the ghost of the gambler who was supposed to be buried with the treasure scare him to death? It's possible, but apparently not even death was enough to cure his obsession. Old Man Crane's ghost is periodically reported to leave the graveyard behind the church on Stonehouse Plains—seemingly still bent on finding the treasure.

The Ghost That Protects Rattlesnakes

There's an old legend in Warren County, in northwest New Jersey, about a ghost that protects people from rattlesnakes and rattlesnakes from people. This ghost appears to warn unwary hikers in the mountains of nearby rattlers, seeming as concerned about the survival of the snakes as for the welfare of people about to encounter one.

Count Zinzendorf, a wealthy German aristocrat, became a missionary to "heathen" Indians early in the nineteenth century, traveling all the way to the wilds of the Appalachians to fulfill his life's work. It is said that he was a dedicated, somewhat aggressive preacher who wouldn't take no for an answer, and that he would follow prospective converts right into their camps and even directly appeal to women and children. He wandered fearlessly on the frontier and was often the first white man to converse with some of the Indians who lived there.

Some Indians became convinced that the count was a spy sent to assess their number, weapons, and determination to resist white settlement. They decided to kill him, but it had to be done quietly. Zinzendorf must be made to just disappear, lest a new Indian war break out.

A band of warriors determined to sneak up on the missionary while he was asleep in his camp. The count had built a fire, as it was a cold night. He was sleeping so soundly that a large rattler, in crawling close to the fire to warm its cold-blooded body, had actually slithered across the sleeping count. When the Indians stealthily approached, they saw the deadly snake and backed off. They interpreted the snake's presence as a sign that the Great Spirit had placed Count Zinzendorf under his protection.

The count lived on for many more years and was regarded as one of the most effective missionaries ever in that region. He found new respect from the local Indians, eventually learning from his hosts that he was under the protection of rattlesnakes and therefore led a charmed life.

In gratitude, the count's spirit appears when a human-rattlesnake encounter might cause the death of either one. If you're hiking in Warren County, watch out for the snakes, and watch out for the count.

Uncle Phillip Turns the Tables

Up in Branchville in Sussex County once lived a rather strange man, almost a hermit, known as "Uncle Phillip." He lived alone on a backwoods farm, making a poor living and earning a certain reputation for himself among his neighbors. Uncle Phillip may have been a little "touched in the head," as the locals say. He never harmed anyone, but his behavior was, well, weird. He fervently believed in ghosts, witches, and goblins of every description. Whatever bad luck he experienced, he blamed on witches. Did his corn crop fail? The witches did it. Did his cow sicken and die? Witchcraft! Did his dog suddenly bite him? It was bewitched. It got to the point where Uncle Phillip wouldn't shake hands, as it might allow an evil spirit to enter him. He expressed fear of cats, as everyone knew that they might be the imps or familiars of witches. If he had a bad night's sleep, it was because ghosts were haunting him.

As kids will, the neighborhood boys played tricks on the lonely old man. They would sneak up on his cabin late at night and make strange sounds. They would steal ripening fruit from his orchard and fields. Tall, gaunt, grouchy Uncle Phillip was the perfect target for this harassment. He'd complain about being bewitched and warn his neighbors about ghosts and monsters of supernatural origin, all to the amusement of the children.

And then Uncle Phillip died, and the harassment tactics began to be visited upon his neighbors, especially victimizing the boys who'd once bothered him. Uncle Phillip's ghost now made life miserable for his former tormentors, turning the tables against the tricksters. To this day, parents in this area warn their children, "Watch out, or Uncle Phillip will get you!"

Communicating with the Dead?

Thomas Edison is credited by some sources with creating—or at least, attempting to create—a device that would allow people in this world to talk to those in the next. However, Douglas G. Tarr, a National Park Service archives technician who works at the Edison National Historic Site, provided copies of correspondence as evidence that the "machine" never developed past the discussion stage. No plans are known to exist or to ever have existed. Tarr has spent more than a decade responding to such inquiries made to the site.

The National Park Service owns and operates the Edison National Historic Site in West Orange, which includes Edison's home, his laboratories, and a replica of the Black Maria, the world's first motion picture studio. Edison constructed this new facility in 1887 on the heels of his stunning successes, including the phonograph and the first practical incandescent light, developed at Menlo Park.

Unlike some of his contemporaries, Edison rarely met a problem that he did not feel equipped to solve. That included his approach to the subject of an afterlife. The origin of his supposed efforts to communicate with the dead apparently started with an article written by B. C. Forbes for *American Magazine* in October 1920. Titled "Edison Working on How to Communicate with the Next World," the story included Edison's description of what he referred to as "life units":

> I believe [our bodies] are composed of myriads and myriads of infinitesimally small individuals, each in itself a unit of life, and that these units work in squads—or swarms, as I prefer to call them—and that these infinitesimally small units live forever. When we "die" these swarms of units, like a swarm of bees, so to speak, betake themselves elsewhere, and go on functioning in some other form or environment.
>
> These life units are, of course, so infinitely small that probably a thousand of them aggregated together would not become visible under even the ultra-microscope, the most powerful magnifying instrument yet invented and constructed by man. These units, if they are as tiny as I believe them to be, would pass through a wall of stone or concrete almost as easily as they would pass through the air.

Edison went on to elaborate on what he believed happened to the "life units" when an individual dies:

Now to return to what is called "life after death." If the units of life which compose an individual's memory hold together after that individual's "death," is it not within the range of possibility, to say the least, that these memory swarms could retain the powers they formerly possessed, and thus retain what we call the individual's personality after "dissolution" of the body? If so, then that individual's memory, or personality, ought to be able to function as before.

I am hopeful, therefore, that by providing the right kind of instrument, to be operated by this personality, we can receive intelligent messages from it in its changed habitation, or environment.

The article closed with Edison shaking a warning finger, declaring: "Mind you, I am promising no results. All I promise is that I will make it easier than it has ever been heretofore for personalities who have 'passed on' to communicate with us, if they are so circumstanced that they can or want to communicate with us."

This interview generated a lot of public interest, since Edison was America's premier inventor at the time, and many around the world regarded him as a virtual magician. After the story broke, he received letters of inquiry from throughout the United States and even one in August 1921 from the Nawab Saheb Bahadur of Palanpur, India, a member of the royal family. Edison's staff responded that the inventor was not yet working on such a machine. The following month, they wrote back to a man in Texas "Mr. Edison desires us to say that he has not yet had time to work on the apparatus to the extent that he would like." Did they mean the Wizard of Menlo Park did, in fact, have such a design up his sleeve? It's unlikely, because the letter continued: "You have misunderstood the reports in newspapers. He is not endeavoring to communicate with departed spirits, nor has he any idea of doing so."

The legend persisted despite such protests, perhaps fueled by a renewed national interest in spiritualism. During the Great Depression, fundamentalist preachers like Amy Semple MacPherson persuaded the poor and homeless that a better life awaited them on "the other side." However, in an October 15, 1926, interview for the *New York Times*, Edison admitted that the author of the original interview, which had generated so much attention, had caught him on a bad day: "I really had nothing to tell him, but I hated to disappoint him, so I thought up this story about communicating with spirits, but it was all a joke."

Lucy Awaits Her True Love

Some local residents around a small northern New Jersey town swear that they have seen Lucy's ghost waiting patiently at the now-disused train station, peering into the growing dusk, waiting for her lover's train to arrive, as it often did during his later life. It is certain that she appreciated the gallant, if somewhat risky, gesture of her one true love in coming to visit her, for he had much to lose if their continuing love affair had become known.

Lucy had been born to a socially prominent but impoverished family. Well-educated and with a charming, poised personality, the beautiful but poor young woman was forced to go to work for $25 a week as the social secretary to the wife of a minor government official in Washington, D.C., during World War I. She soon caught the eye of her employer's husband, an outgoing, independently wealthy, and very ambitious official in the Department of the Navy. Soon, as her employer later discovered to her dismay, Lucy was registering at secluded hotels as her lover's "wife," and an intense love affair had begun. But Lucy was a devout Catholic, who would have had serious questions about marrying a divorced man, even if a divorce was likely. It was not.

Her lover was very reluctant to leave his wife and five children. Lucy was well aware that her first and greatest love was offered a divorce by his outraged wife, but that his mother had threatened to cut her only son off without a penny—and he had little money of his own—if he divorced. The boyfriend's wife and mother both demanded that the affair with the lovely social secretary end permanently.

Lucy found another job, as governess to a wealthy New Jersey widower with five children to raise. Lucy soon married her employer, Winthrop Rutherfurd, who, at age fifty-eight, was exactly twice Lucy's age of twenty-nine. When her husband died in his old age, Lucy became very wealthy, richer by far than her true love.

Their relationship flourished in secrecy for the rest of his life. They met whenever his wife was out of town, which, fortunately for the lovers, was frequent. After Lucy Rutherfurd was widowed, her lover made a habit of detouring to visit Lucy in her North Jersey home when on his way from his office to weekend visits to his boyhood home in New York's Hudson Valley. That is where the tiny, seldom-used train station near Lucy's home came in. Lucy's lover was by now important enough that his special train would stop anyplace he chose.

Lucy really looked forward to those occasions when her long-time lover's train stopped just for him and her, to rekindle a lifelong love affair at considerable risk to his reputation. It must have been a spectacular as well as joyous time when the heavily armored rail-car, *Ferdinand Magellan*, the private car of President Franklin D. Roosevelt, pulled slowly into the little whistle-stop station for another secret rendezvous.

Lucy's ghost still visits the trackside where the most important man in the world at the time risked public ridicule just to spend a few hours with her in her country home. No wonder her spirit still occasionally peers down the track, anticipating another meeting.

The Philadelphia Experiment

Although it was known as the Philadelphia Experiment, the secret government project that was developed during World War II had several New Jersey connections. The Philadelphia Experiment reportedly began in 1943 when the U.S. Navy wanted to demagnetize its warships. The official story was that this process would reduce their exposure to the enemy's radar. However, some believe that there was a little more to the project than that official explanation.

Was the Navy actually working to create an invisible fleet? Were their efforts successful? And, as an unexpected benefit, did they develop ships that could travel not just safely through water, but through time as well?

The Philadelphia Experiment was started because the Navy reportedly was losing too many ships to a new type of Nazi mine that was drawn to the partially magnetized ship hulls. By demagnetizing the ships, they would become virtually invisible to this type of attack. At the same time, Navy officials were concerned that the atomic bomb would not be an effective deterrent to the Japanese during World War II. They thought it would require a full assault on the islands of Japan to end the war and wanted their fleet to be fully prepared in the event the ships were needed to carry and protect an invasion force of troops.

Navy officials contacted a group of scientists at Princeton University, which included Albert Einstein, and asked for their assistance in developing a successful method of degaussing (demagnetizing) ships. Some ambitious young physicists working at the university reportedly decided to take advantage of the opportunity to not only address the Navy's problem, but also resolve a few concerns of their own, which involved time displacement through the use of magnetic fields. It is not known whether Einstein was involved with the Philadelphia Experiment, but he reportedly was under contract to the Navy during the war years.

The physicists who were employed by the Navy worked primarily out of the Philadelphia Naval Shipyard. The test craft was the 1,240-ton *Cannon* class destroyer that eventually would be christened the USS *Eldridge*. Bill Knell, in "The Philadelphia Experiment: Sixty Years Later," wrote of the first experiments conducted in 1943:

> A powerful electromagnetic field was used to instantly degauss the ship without any damage to electronic equipment on board. The vessel also became invisible to radar, but an unexpected and more than welcomed side effect occurred that the scientists hoped for, but the Navy didn't expect. It briefly vanished from sight, becoming what the observers had thought was invisible.

A bright greenish glow had been observed both before the ship disappeared and after it returned. Further study led the scientists to believe that the ship had vanished from sight because it briefly jumped through time to another location. Although some small animals placed on board died mysteriously during the test, Navy officials reportedly were pleased enough with the results to authorize further work on the project.

In 1944, a sea trial was conducted off the coast of New Jersey. The *Eldridge* was manned and set sail, surrounded by a number of other ships that carried the same equipment. The Navy hoped that they would successfully bypass any radar or sonar that enemy ships and submarines might be using in the region. However, while the other ships were able to successfully power their generators, the *Eldridge* began to once again emit a strange green glow when its generator was started, then abruptly vanished from sight.

The USS *Eldridge* reportedly appeared in 1983 off the coast of Long Island just moments after the time it had vanished on the same calendar date thirty-nine years earlier, allegedly traveling through a "worm hole" created by simultaneous experiments with time travel at Philadelphia and at Montauk Point. Seconds later, the ship was pulled back to 1944 when the Montauk experiment was shut down. It was said that some crewmembers died during the test run and that the remaining sailors, traumatized by the experience, were locked away in the mental ward of a Navy hospital for the rest of their lives.

At the same time that the *Eldridge* supposedly appeared near Long Island, another report filed by the crew of the civilian merchant ship SS *Andrew Furuseth* stated that they observed the arrival of the *Eldridge* off the coast of Norfolk, Virginia. However, Lieutenant Junior Grade William S. Dodge, of the U.S. Naval Reserves, who was master of the *Furuseth* at that time, later denied this statement in writing.

Despite the experience, the *Eldridge* was considered seaworthy. Following the trial run, it joined other American destroyers in Europe, where it remained stationed for the duration of the war. The ship was later decommissioned and sent to Greece, where it was rechristened the *Leon* (Lion) and served as part of the Greek Navy into the 1990s. Although the USS *Eldridge*'s role in the Philadelphia Experiment has been the focus of discussion for many years, to date, no one has ever satisfactorily resolved the question of what happened to the ship and its crew when it first set out to sea. The Navy isn't talking.

Domestic Ghosts

Ginny's Gin House, a centuries-old restaurant near Pleasant City that was once a hotel, then later a stagecoach stop and a brothel, is reportedly haunted by a variety of domestic ghosts. Like many spirits who lived before modern technology, Ginny's ghosts are apparently fascinated by contemporary household conveniences. The spirits, both male and female, spend their time running faucets and flushing toilets when they're not vacuuming the restaurant floors.

Although it might seem strange to think that someone would pass up the chance at a more peaceful afterlife to perform housework, the ghosts have their reasons for performing these chores. When a past owner held a séance to communicate with the phantoms, he learned they were simply trying to help out because they had once owned the business located there and felt an obligation to ensure that their successors enjoyed continued success.

New Jersey

THE OLDEST STORIES OF UNEXPLAINED PHENOMENA FROM CENTRAL NEW Jersey came from the Unami, the Lenni-Lenape tribe that lived in that part of the state. The Unami believed the world was once completely covered by water. Then a great tortoise arose from beneath the water, and as the waters receded, his shell became dry land. Before long, a tree sprouted on the surface of the newly risen earth, and from the slender branches of the tree grew first a man, then a woman. These two people were the parents of all the people who came afterward on earth. As a result of his role in creating the world, the tortoise was always respectfully addressed as "Grandfather." Any time an earthquake shook the ground, the Unami believed the tortoise was moving. What is especially interesting about this story is that scientists later discovered that the Pine Barrens, which cover a large portion of the center of the state, were in fact immersed before subterranean shifts forced the land up from beneath the water.

Other Unami deities included Mother Corn, an old woman who lived far, far away and was responsible for all growing things on the earth. Snow Boy controlled ice and snow. Living Solid Face was a healer who protected the animals of the forest. The Unami sometimes claimed to have seen this masked being riding a buck and herding deer, his face painted black on one side and red on the other. The Unami made regular offerings to all these supernatural beings to ensure the tribe's continued health and well-being.

The Burrowes Tragedy

The town of Matawan, which traces its roots to Colonial America, was once the home of John "Corn King" Burrowes, a wealthy merchant who made his fortune transporting produce with a fleet of sailing ships to towns along the eastern seaboard. Like many successful entrepreneurs of the time, Burrowes built an elegant mansion in the picturesque community and looked forward to enjoying a life of peace and prosperity with his family.

But like so many others, the Burrowes clan eventually found their lives disrupted by the advent of war. Unlike some New Jersey families, however, they had no difficulty deciding which cause to support. John Burrowes Jr. was appointed a major in the American Army. Together with his future brother-in-law, Jonathan Forman, he organized New Jersey's first militia company in the garden of his father's home.

The Corn King, a shrewd businessman, had well-stocked granaries when war broke out and before long was the envy of his loyalist neighbors. When food shortages became common, the British supporters decided to make the rebel Burrowes pay for his good fortune. One night, when his son had unexpectedly arrived home for a surprise visit with his wife, Burrowes was warned that British troops were on their way to capture the younger man. As the soldiers fought allies of the Burrowes family who were blocking their way, John Jr. made his escape. But the British soldiers were determined to take their revenge.

They broke into the house and, after a cursory search, discovered the major had escaped. As they gathered in the entryway to the house, one soldier demanded that Margaret Forman Burrowes, the major's wife, give up her shawl to stanch the wounds of an officer who had been injured during the fighting. Standing on the elegant wooden staircase at the center of the main hall, Margaret declared that she would never part with her shawl for such a purpose. Angered by her words, the soldier thrust his bayonet into her, fatally wounding the young woman, who died almost immediately.

Although the outbuildings were destroyed that fateful night, the mansion remained untouched, perhaps out of respect for the young woman who was willing to sacrifice her life for her principles, or perhaps because shortly after her death, Margaret's spirit was reportedly seen flickering protectively around the front hall, determined to keep all invaders at bay. Whatever the reason, the house survived the ravages of war and time. It was restored in the 1990s and today is a museum of local history owned and maintained by the Matawan Historic Sites Commission.

Hannah Caldwell

Hannah Caldwell was another casualty of the Revolutionary War, whose death incited residents of Connecticut Farms, known today as Union, to fight even harder against British troops. She was the wife of Rev. James Caldwell, who served as minister of the local Presbyterian church around 1780. When fighting broke out in the region, the reverend enlisted with the American Army. To ensure his family's safety, he took Hannah and their young children to a rectory about five miles away. However, a lone British soldier who was trespassing through the rectory garden caught sight of Hannah in a window. He fired a single shot, instantly killing her. British troops later returned and burned the rectory to the ground. The date was June 7, 1780.

When Reverend Caldwell heard the news, he raced home from the battlefield, only to discover the body of his wife lying in the ashes and his crying children waiting near the ruined house. After burying Hannah and delivering his children into the care of a friend, Caldwell returned and rallied the troops to victory in what was later known as the Battle of Springfield. Although the Americans were less in number and poorly equipped, they were inspired by the reverend and managed to defeat the British.

Today local residents have reported seeing the ghost of a woman wearing Colonial dress haunting the First Presbyterian Churchyard in Elizabeth, where she is buried. Hannah's ghost has also been seen in other parts of the region, probably searching for her beloved husband, who died a year later fighting for his country.

The Ghosts of Aaron Burr, Father and Son

Aaron Burr, second vice president of the United States, senator, governor of New York, adventurer, womanizer, killer of Alexander Hamilton, and alleged traitor, was a New Jerseyan, born in Newark.

One of the most controversial American politicians, he is buried at Princeton, next to his father of the same name. Two men more different than father and son would be hard to imagine. Even their ghosts are opposites.

The first Aaron Burr was a highly respectable, and respected, citizen. A Presbyterian minister, he became the second president of the College of New Jersey in 1747. Under Burr's leadership, the young college moved from Elizabethtown to Newark to Princeton, where it found a permanent home and a new name—Princeton University.

No sooner had the move to Princeton and into Nassau Hall, the college's new building, been accomplished, than the Reverend Burr died in 1757, at the age of forty-two. He left behind an infant son, also named Aaron. By the time he was three, young Aaron had lost both parents and inherited a nice sum of money. Ambitious, bright, and hardworking, this Aaron Burr graduated from Princeton at the age of sixteen.

Burr served honorably in the American Revolution as a colonel, emerging with a much better reputation than his onetime commanding officer, Benedict Arnold. To his great disgust, he lost a very close election to Thomas Jefferson. Coming in second in those days made you vice president, a job that Burr hated. Burr became involved in a plot to create a new empire from the part of the United States west of the Appalachians, with a capital at New Orleans. Tried for treason in 1807, he was not convicted, due to lack of evidence. But everyone knew he was a liar and a schemer. Actually, Burr's reputation had gone steadily downhill after his famous duel with his political archrival Alexander Hamilton.

Burr shot Hamilton at Weehawken, New Jersey, on July 11, 1804. Burr had insisted on a duel; Hamilton reluctantly agreed because he refused to apologize for publicly criticizing Burr's lack of morals, personally and politically. It is said that Hamilton, who fired simultaneously with Burr, aimed to miss. Burr did not. He was accused of murder, but New Jersey did not prosecute him.

Aaron Burr also was a notorious womanizer. It was said of him that the pursuit of the opposite sex absorbed all his thoughts.

Today the bodies of father and son lie side by side in a Princeton cemetery. Both men's spirits are prone to roaming about. The elder Aaron Burr is a quiet, thoughtful, and unobtrusive ghost, haunting Nassau Hall and checking up on the progress of his beloved college. His son's ghost wanders about in search of attractive ladies to seduce and is said to have been positively delighted, and to have become much more active, when Princeton University went coed in the 1960s.

Bad Vibrations

A mansion in the town of Cranberry once served as temporary residence to a number of prominent men who played important roles in the Revolutionary War. Washington, Jefferson, and Hamilton were some of the guests who stayed in the pre-Revolutionary home that occupied a corner of New Brunswick Pike and King George's Highway.

Following the war years, the house was purchased by Commodore Truxton, who had served in the U.S. Navy. Not long afterward, it briefly became the home of the infamous Aaron Burr, who was fleeing after his duel with Alexander Hamilton. Truxton, a friend of Burr's, reluctantly allowed Burr to stay in a room on the top floor of the mansion that could be reached only by a hidden staircase. According to Charles M. Skinner in *American Myths and Legends,* "He came out only by night, and took the air in the heavy shade of trees." Burr soon fled the country, but some of his malicious spirit seemed to remain behind to permeate the mansion. When Truxton was forced to move away after unsuccessfully speculating with his fortune and losing everything, the ensuing owners never seemed to enjoy their new abode for very long.

A judge whose harsh punishments made him generally hated by the local population lived briefly in the house. The local population came to believe that the house's essence influenced his sentences, which became heavier each time he went to court. A Quaker who was more than a few years older than his wife watched in dismay as the young woman became an opium addict after they moved in. Although he tried everything to force her to stop using drugs, his wife managed to enlist the aid of neighborhood children and servants, who smuggled opium into the house. The young woman eventually killed herself in Burr's secret room on the third floor.

After the Quaker lost his fortune, he sold the house and it rapidly changed hands in the years that followed. A slaveowner, a retired Army officer, a physician, and a financier all experienced

loss and misfortune after moving into the mansion. The last owners, a distiller and his wife, both died of hemorrhages within days
of each other. Local residents used to claim that after the house
was finally vacated, a few brave curiosity seekers who entered the
building could hear footsteps on the hidden staircase leading to
Burr's third-floor room. Shadows of human figures would appear
on the walls when no person stood nearby. Few people willingly
entered the mansion, however, because they believed that Burr's
restless spirit wanted to make sure others were afflicted with the
same adversity that he felt he had suffered in life.

A Family of Ghosts

The ghosts of a South Branch family once haunted a three-story
Victorian house on South Branch River Road across from the Stud-
derford Bridge. According to local legend, the entire family who
had resided there was murdered in the old post office that once
stood next door. The house, which dated from the Civil War, was
torn down in the late 1970s. But before it was destroyed, locals
reported a variety of strange occurrences that happened to the families who tried to live there—the vacuum cleaner would turn on
and move by itself, the furniture shifted around on its own, door
handles rattled, and curtains swayed in an unseen breeze. One family's German shepherd reportedly cowered so badly whenever it
had to enter the house that they finally had to send it to a new
home. No family stayed very long in the old house haunted by an
entire family of ghosts. Did the family that died together stay
together as spirits? Local residents said that lights continued to be
seen moving through the upper levels of the house long after it was
vacated, but that there has been no apparent supernatural activity
in the area since the house was destroyed.

A Brotherly Argument

At the Presbyterian Cemetery in Springfield, near Union, two ghosts
clad in soldiers' uniforms have been observed sitting side by side on
their neighboring tombstones, having a friendly argument. If anyone is brave enough to approach them, they simply fade from sight.
When the tombstones are examined (full daylight seems to be safe),

it is revealed that they belong to two brothers, Elias and William Poole, who are buried next to one another. Both brothers served honorably in the Civil War, and both survived the war. The older brother, Elias, was an artilleryman; his younger brother, William, was in the infantry of the Grand Army of the Potomac.

So what are they still arguing about after all these years? Politics, perhaps, for while William's grave is decorated every Memorial Day with the stars and stripes of a valiant soldier, Elias's matching tombstone is topped with the stars and bars of the Confederacy. Elias had fought for a Virginia regiment, having gone south before the war to look for work.

Babe in the Woods

One of the saddest ghost stories told by New Jerseyans is that of the lost child in the woods. It seems that on early spring mornings, when a ground mist hugs the woods, the trees just beginning to show light green buds, the pale ghost of a small child appears. This has been reported along lonely roads in the general vicinity of Princeton.

First the faint sound of a toddler's voice is heard. "Mommy? Daddy?" pleads the tearful little voice in the woods. Soon after, it has been reported, a glimpse of the source of the plaintive calls is seen: a handsome, blue-eyed little boy with curly golden hair, worn longer than in present fashion. The child is wearing a one-piece white cotton coverall, the kind with "footies" attached.

But why would a toddler, obviously dressed for bed, be wandering about in the cool, damp woods? What is particularly interesting is that the pathetic little ghost perfectly fits the description of Charles A. Lindbergh Jr., the kidnapped son of the world-famous pioneer aviator. The little boy probably was smothered during the kidnapping from his home in nearby Hopewell on March 1, 1932. His grief-stricken parents soon afterward left New Jersey to spend much of their later lives far away, in England at first, then in Hawaii.

UFOs in New Jersey?

Long before the supposed UFO crash in Roswell, New Mexico, it long will be remembered that many New Jersey citizens, at least briefly, were believers in the possibility of alien invasion when they had a "close encounter" with Martians. The year was 1938, when popular radio and film personality Orson Welles broadcast "War of the Worlds," an updated version of the classic H. G. Wells story about an alien invasion of earth.

Les Krantz, in *America by the Numbers,* noted that the broadcast was originally intended as a Halloween treat for radio listeners, on Sunday night, October 30, 1938, "it was reported that a huge, falling object had fallen on the Wilmuth Farm near Grovers Mill, New Jersey, a small town not far from Trenton." Welles and the cast of the Mercury Theater in New York City apparently threw such passion into the presentation that they created hysteria not just in New Jersey, but throughout the nation. Americans became convinced that the National Guard and the Army were being mobilized to fight the Martian invaders, who were described in dramatic detail: "There seemed to be tentacles. The eyes were black and reptilian; the V-shaped mouth quivered and dripped saliva." Evening church services throughout Trenton became "end of the world" prayer meetings.

Later studies of the event revealed that Welles apparently had touched a nerve in the collective American conscious. The program probably would not have received such attention if there hadn't been a certain amount of prewar hysteria about Nazi activities in Europe. And the airship *Hindenburg* had exploded the previous year in Lakewood, leaving New Jersey residents fearful of German technology and the effects it could have on their lives.

Have UFOs been visiting the earth since the dawn of civilization? Unbelievers mock the idea of little gray folk who are consistently described as having large heads, saucerlike black eyes, and the ability to manipulate human behavior. Whether you believe or not, one thing is indisputably true—the topic has haunted humankind for generations. In the United States, there has been a lively debate about visitors from outer space since 1948, when many believed a spaceship crashed outside of Roswell, New Mexico. In recent years, a spate of television shows and movies has revived interest in the subject.

One Vineland woman recalled:

Even though it's been more than twenty-five years, I still get chills when I think about that night I saw the UFO. It was a brisk, cold February in 1975. I had forgotten to take out the trash after dinner, so there I was, putting on my shoes at close to midnight to wrestle the cans out to the end of the driveway. After I set the second can by the side of the road, I was prepared to do a little stargazing. This was back at a time before security lights, and you could still see the night sky. But when I turned around, I discovered the sky was "gazing" at me. There it was—hovering silently about twenty feet above the maple tree in our front yard. My jaw dropped. It was triangle-shaped and the bottom was covered with row upon row of white lights, and it just hung there like the world's largest Christmas tree ornament.

I wanted to scream, I wanted to cry out, to make some kind of noise to get the others in the house out, so that they could see it too. But the most noise I could make was a little squeak, and it felt like I had suddenly grown roots into the driveway. I don't know how long I stood there, frozen in the yard, but suddenly I was able to run, and boy did I run. However, in the time it took me to cross the driveway and get into the house, crying out for the others to come and see, the thing virtually disappeared. As I looked out the front windows, all I could see was a brilliant light moving south for a few seconds. Then it was gone.

According to Les Krantz in *America by the Numbers,* authorities receive about ten thousand reports each year from anxious Americans who claim to have spotted a UFO. A staggering 25 million people believe they have had a close encounter of some kind. According to a Roper poll, at least 3.75 million men and women, from a variety of ethnic and economic backgrounds, believe they've been abducted by aliens.

Today Grovers Mills is no longer on any New Jersey map. But for some Garden State residents, the memory of that frightening night when the Martians were said to have landed lingers on.

The Duck Island Killer

Its official name was Duck Island, but to many residents of Hamilton Township in the late 1930s, it was well known as the local "lovers lane." Over the years, teenage and adult couples frequented the secluded peninsula in search of privacy, but in 1939, these liaisons came abruptly to an end. That was the year the "Duck Island Killer," as he was dubbed by the local newspapers, was identified as the serial murderer behind a three-year rampage that resulted in the death of at least six people.

On September 30, 1939, his victims were twenty-eight-year-old Frank Kasper of Trenton, a husband and father, and Katherine Werner, thirty-six, a homemaker who lived nearby. Their illicit rendezvous that night at Duck Island wasn't their first, but it would prove to be their last. The couple may have hidden their relationship from their families, but they were discovered by a man armed with a shotgun who stepped from the trees and, with three quick shots, killed the couple.

When police arrived on the scene the following morning, they realized that the crime was very similar to another that had occurred the previous year, in almost the same location. In 1938, Vincenzo "Jim" Tonzillo, a married man, had been having an affair with fifteen-year-old Mary Myatovich, and they frequently parked at Duck Island. Tonzillo was killed immediately by a shotgun blast, but Myatovich lingered for two days in a local hospital. She recounted that she had been sexually assaulted by the mysterious attacker after he shot her, but she was unable to offer police much of a description of her assailant before she died.

While authorities began their manhunt after the second couple was murdered, the local newspapers described the killings in lurid detail. Many lovers throughout Hamilton Township soon realized that they needed to find another secret meeting place. According to Jon Black in an article in the *Trentonian:* "For three more years, he would prowl the lovers lanes of Hamilton Township and Bucks County, Pa. He might steal something—but mostly, he just wanted to kill." The following winter, the Duck Island Killer struck again, killing Louis Kovacs and Carolina Morconi, two lovers who again wanted to hide their affair from the world.

On April 7, 1942, the killer assaulted another couple in Pennsylvania, but they miraculously survived and were able to provide police with further information. A few months later, authorities arrested Clarence Hill, a married laborer whose outward respectability hid a monster capable of sexual assault and murder. When he was brought to trial, Hill was quickly found guilty and sentenced to life in prison. He served less than twenty years, and after his release, he lived quietly by all accounts. Hill died of natural causes on July 9, 1973. However, to this day, most Hamilton Township residents no longer rendezvous on Duck Island. The restless spirits of the murder victims finally have all the privacy they could desire.

Southern New Jersey

SOUTH JERSEY IS KNOWN FOR ITS GHOST TOWNS, WHICH TODAY REALLY are ghosts themselves, as it's hard to find traces of most of them. Forget the mental image of ghost towns of the Old West—picturesque, largely intact buildings preserved in remote deserts and high mountains. The New Jersey Pinelands' ghost towns have suffered a longer period of neglect than most western ghost towns. Vandals, forest fires, and souvenir hunters all have taken their toll on Pinelands ghost towns. In South Jersey today, only the ghosts are left, along with the Jersey Devil and some other mysterious phenomena.

Ghost Towns of the Pinelands

For the same reason that the more famous ghost towns of the West came to be, South Jersey has many ghost towns, and these ghost towns often have resident ghosts. Ghost towns are abandoned, at least by their living residents, because their economic base disappears, as so often happens when a mine is exhausted.

How can New Jersey, statistically the most crowded state in the Union, have ghost towns? The changing fortunes of the iron industry in the Pinelands explains most of the abandoned communities that make South Jersey the eastern United States' ghost town capital.

While the north-central Highlands of the state boasted many iron mines, furnaces, and forges, that industry was based on "black rock" magnetic ores, which are of high quality and present in such quantity that iron mining continues there up to the present. The Pinelands furnaces, and there were many of them, were based on bog ore, a lower-quality ore present in smaller quantities.

Also, in both Highlands and Pinelands, charcoal was the preferred fuel for smelting ores in the early years. But charcoal, made by roasting wood in earth-covered mounds, used up enormous quantities of wood. The Highlands furnaces were close to the Pennsylvania hard coal mines, which supplied a superior substitute for charcoal. The Pinelands furnaces lacked cheap transport to bring in coal, so South Jersey's furnaces eventually ran out of both ore and fuel.

Imagine the plight of the South Jersey ironworkers. In the Colonial period, and especially during the Revolution, their products were much in demand. Their cannons and cannonballs were vital in winning America's freedom. In the first half of the nineteenth century, New Jersey was the third most important iron-producing state. In the Southern Pines, iron centers like Weymouth, Atsion, Hampton Furnace, Mary Ann Furnace, Batsto, and Martha's Furnace, once thriving, are now all but gone—a collection of memories and entries in the history books. State restoration and preservation efforts help keep a few, like Batsto Village, on the map as tourist attractions.

Through no fault of their own, as their products were acknowledged to be of high quality, the ironmasters were forced out of business by events far away and beyond their control. Pennsylvania coal, Great Lakes iron ores, new technologies—all of these events led to the once bustling little communities dying as surely as the fires died out in the furnaces.

King of the Woods: The Jersey Devil

As anyone who has ever traveled through the Pine Barrens knows, the forest can be a frightening place, especially after dark. You might be less than a half hour from home, with your favorite radio station playing loud and clear, but the tall, endless sea of trees beneath a pitch black sky can make it seem like you've stepped back into another world where strange beings roam the night.

One restless creature that has haunted the New Jersey Pine Barrens for almost two centuries is the well-known Jersey Devil. While some of the earliest stories pinpoint his birth at Leeds Point along the shore, he may have been born in Pleasantville or Estelville. Although his mother was human, his father was reportedly none other than Satan himself. The Jersey Devil was said to have been the thirteenth—and most unwelcome—child of either the Leeds or Shourds family. Exhausted by the pain of constant childbirth, the mother cursed the child as it was being born. However, she was shocked when the midwife delivered a baby that was far from human.

Over the years, the creature has been described as having the head of a horse or cow, a body like a kangaroo or a horse, and feet like a pig. Some describe him with the talons of an eagle, but others say he inherited his father's cloven hooves. As the legend goes, the Jersey Devil escaped from his home immediately after birth either through an open window or up a chimney. Although some claim that the young monster's first meal consisted of his twelve older siblings, most people don't believe the Devil has ever attacked a human being. Over the years, he reportedly has killed chickens and other farm animals and has been seen by travelers, prowling the region at night.

A far older version of the Devil's origins dates to the Lenni-Lenape, the local Native Americans whose traditions included a mysterious "night monster," who would appear on occasion to terrify villagers and frighten away game animals. Children were told never to venture into the woods after dark because the night monster might catch and eat them. The more common story, however, is that the Jersey Devil was the child of a European immigrant who arrived in New Jersey in the eighteenth century.

The first published account of the Jersey Devil, titled "In the Pines" in the *Atlantic Monthly* in 1859, stated that the child was born human, but "no sooner did he see the light than he assumed the form of a fiend, with a horse's head, wings of a bat, and a serpent's tail." Since that time, his activities have been recorded in newspapers, periodicals, and folktales. The Devil reportedly has been seen throughout South Jersey, from Pleasantville to Salem and many points in between. Some claim that he usually appears whenever the threat of war is in the air. In the mid-1970s, it was even claimed that he had been seen in Texas, although most New

Jersey residents doubt that the creature would have strayed that far from home. In 1939, a New Jersey guidebook listed the Phantom of the Pines as the official "state demon." The 1976 book *The Jersey Devil*, by James F. McCloy and Ray Miller Jr., has remained so popular that it is now in its fifteenth printing. In 2001, the first full-length feature film made in 2001 about the Jersey Devil, titled *The Thirteenth Child: The Legend of the Jersey Devil, Volume I*, was released. Unfortunately, it completely lost sight of the original myth and became just another B-grade horror movie.

Thanks to all this public attention, the Jersey Devil has lived a long and healthy life and is the best-known New Jersey myth. One of the primary reasons he has stuck around so long may be because he apparently helped keep outsiders from uncovering some of the secrets that lay hidden within the Pine Barrens. During the Revolutionary War, he may have kept British troops from investigating any suspicious lights or noises that they saw in the night. It is said that the locals, tired of his mischief, hired an itinerant preacher to exorcise the Jersey Devil, who was cast out of the woods for one hundred years. When he returned, the Devil reportedly wreaked havoc for weeks, as though punishing Pinelands residents for what he perceived as their betrayal.

With the advent of Prohibition, crude stills spread throughout the forest produced Jersey's own version of "white lightning," which was sold from the back of old Model Ts to individuals and restaurants in the region. Residents of the Pine Barrens, who also depended heavily on a steady supply of fish and game to feed their families during those lean years, might also have spread the tale to discourage sportsmen from hunting in their woods.

Although no one has reported sighting the Jersey Devil recently, tales occasionally do surface about encounters. One such story, handed down through a local family, relates the saga of a close encounter with the Phantom of the Pines:

> According to my father, Uncle Fred used to run moonshine in and out of the Pine Barrens back in the 1930s in an old Model T truck that was held together with a strong rope and a length of chain. Well, the story goes that one night, in the fall of 1931—one of the last years of Prohibition—Fred was on his way back to town with a truckload of moonshine from a bootlegger he knew. Like everybody else, Fred needed money. Since many Americans needed a drink,

despite a government that said they couldn't have one, Fred saw an answer to his problem.

Like most people born and raised in South Jersey, Fred had heard tales of the Jersey Devil, the strange demon who had terrorized the Pinelands and nearby seashore for nearly two centuries. Although it was probably not a good idea to venture out alone with night coming on, Fred was just a little more afraid of the law than he was of any legend.

The Model T was rattling down a sandy road when he heard an odd noise from the back of the truck. Thinking that maybe the barrels were shifting loose, he glanced in the rearview mirror and was shocked to see an odd-looking figure loping along behind the truck. Although the truck didn't move that fast, Fred was still surprised to see the figure not just keeping up, but getting steadily closer. Fred sped up a little. His follower kept pace. As he watched, he realized with a chill that what he'd thought at first was a jacket blowing out behind the figure was looking more and more like wings. Suddenly the figure loomed directly behind the truck, then alongside it! Fred slammed on the brakes and watched as a long, horselike face grinned at him through the driver's side window, a reddish glow emanating from its eyes. The stranger gave a kind of hop, jump, and skip, then sped ahead of him down the road.

Fred slammed on the brakes and watched with a dropped jaw as its flapping, batlike wings carried it off the ground, and it disappeared from view into the trees. That was Uncle Fred's experience with the Jersey Devil, although in closing, Dad always added with a grin, "Of course, I have to say that your uncle did use to take a sample now and again whenever he was on the road to and from the Pine Barrens."

A Visitor from the West

While the Jersey Devil is the most famous of all New Jersey's monsters, he seems to have developed some competition in recent years. Apparently Bigfoot, although allegedly a denizen of the West, has been sighted at least fourteen times in the Garden State, according to the Bigfoot tracking website. The reports, which come primarily from the Pine Barrens in Burlington County, range from alleged sightings to noises and footprints that were deemed characteristic of the creature.

In 1997, thirty campers participated in a three-day hike on the Batona Trail, a path that winds through the heart of the Pinelands. One restless camper reported that after they had made camp for the night, he was awakened about 1:30 in the morning "by a terrible scream" that was like nothing he had ever heard before. Later that morning, several other hikers admitted that they also had heard the noise but had been too frightened to move or say anything. Such wails and the sound of something large moving through the bushes periodically frighten campers and are believed to be signs of Bigfoot, because he frequents watering places off the beaten track.

Other regions where Bigfoot has been spotted include rural areas of Sussex, Ocean, Middlesex, and Warren Counties. One detailed account was offered by a woman who believed she encountered Bigfoot on a warm summer day in 1970 near the town of Milford. She was about nine years old at the time, visiting an uncle who lived in a wooded rural area. While walking near the stream that ran behind her uncle's house, she heard noises in the brush on the other side of the water. Although she thought at first that it was probably her older brothers, she soon observed a strange figure approaching. The woman recalled: "It appeared to be very big and was covered completely in dark long hair. I thought maybe it was a bear but the face was not like a bear at all."

She continued: "It stopped in front of me and looked directly at me . . . I closed my eyes, held my breath and waited for it to kill me or leave. . . . Thankfully it left, just walked away."

Although many years had passed, the woman clearly recalled how terrified she was of the startling creature. She ran back to her uncle's house, crying, and because she was so frightened, the family moved to a nearby hotel for the remainder of their visit.

Another Monstrous Visitor

Like many other ethnic groups who brought the legends of their various homelands with them to the United States, New Jersey's Puerto Rican community in recent years has shared tales of the creature known as the Chupacabra, or "Goat Sucker." Since the early 1990s, the monster reportedly has appeared in the Pine Barrens and farmlands of South Jersey, where it has attacked farm animals, dogs, and cats.

Although it is usually described as vaguely human in appearance, the Chupacabra emits a strong, sulfuric stench and is also said to have goatlike legs and to be able to change colors like a chameleon in order to blend into its surroundings. It has fiery red eyes and fangs protruding from its slitlike mouth, usually used to bite its victims in the neck. Circular puncture wounds, grouped in triangular patterns, apparently cause instant death. Like the Jersey Devil, "Chupie," as it is sometimes called, reportedly has never killed a human being, but its frightening appearance has startled more than one farmer into reaching for the nearest shotgun.

The Dancing Bandit

In times past, the lonely roads across the Pinelands held more danger than just getting stuck in the loose sand. Highwaymen roamed the narrow old roads through the dense woods, accosting lone travelers with the demand, backed by a gun, "Stand and deliver!" And deliver they would, for this was a case of their money or their life.

The most famous of the early highwaymen was Joe Mulliner, who was active in the 1770s and 1780s, when deserters from both the American and British Armies hid out in the woods and made a living off robberies, smuggling, extortion, and moonshining.

Highwaymen like Joe Mulliner not only robbed travelers, but also extorted "protection money" from local citizens to leave them alone. Tavern owners in particular paid highwaymen not to rob their guests, at least until the guest had paid his bill for lodging, food, and drink. Joe was unique in that he robbed only the rich. If a poor traveler, ordered to stand and deliver, could deliver but a few coins, Joe usually let him keep his money and sent him on his way. Joe also gave money to the poorest of his neighbors, saying it was truly a crime to let a human starve. His generosity to the poor and to church poor boxes made Joe Mulliner a local hero—a sort of homegrown Robin Hood.

Joe was said to have taken a fancy to Honore Read, the beautiful daughter of the ironmaster who lived at Pleasant Mills, near Batsto. Honore knew of Joe's fascination with her, but her rich father was not at all pleased about the charming outlaw's intentions. When Honore was to be the hostess of a great party to celebrate her birthday, the guest list was quite long, but it did not include Joe Mulliner, who definitely expected an invitation. There are two versions of what happened next. According to one source, Joe defiantly crashed the party. He danced with Honore in a whirling dance that gave frustrated onlookers no chance to grab him without endangering his partner. Finally, Joe whirled Honore right out the door, using her as a temporary hostage, then leaped upon his horse and disappeared.

In the second version of the story, Joe kidnapped Honore from her house on the afternoon of the party. Her ransom, as the story went, was his demand of Honore that she, in the delicate language of the day, give him her "wholehearted affection." Whatever took place, Honore was returned safely in time for her party. Neither Joe nor Honore would ever say what persuaded him to let her go free.

Joe was soon afterward captured by a vigilante posse one night at a tavern, which still stands in the tiny rural town of Nesco. Arrowhead Tavern, known today as Indian Cabin Tavern, is distinguished today by a small historical marker that states, "Joseph Mulliner noted refugee—Tory—outlaw captured here in 1781."

Mulliner was tried and sentenced to hang in Burlington, West Jersey's capital at the time, supposedly as an example of the fate that awaited other "gentlemen of the road." According to Henry C. Beck in *Forgotten Towns of Southern New Jersey*, the highwayman was probably "strung up officially at Woodbury gaol," like others before him.

In the 1960s, some local pranksters set up a tombstone in Pleasant Mills that supposedly marked the site of Mulliner's grave. It is more than likely, however, that his body was laid to rest on land along the Mullica River, which was owned by his wife. But his spirit does not rest. "Stand and deliver!" shouts the ghost that some claim to have met on dark nights. At other times, the ghost of Joe Mulliner can be seen spinning his sweetheart about merrily as he dances to ghostly music.

The Pine Robbers

Fenton, Fagan, and Burke. It sounds like a law firm, but it was a kind of outlaw firm in the early nineteenth century. The sparsely populated forests of New Jersey's Pinelands were the refuge of a variety of scoundrels—former pirates, smugglers, runaways, renegade soldiers, moonshiners, and highwaymen. Fenton, Fagan, and Burke were robbers who occasionally hung out with one another and cooperated in illegal activities.

Fenton was a large, powerful man who had been a blacksmith. A man of violent temper, he once robbed a tailor shop of a new suit of clothes. He didn't particularly hide this crime, as he walked around proud of his new outfit. The tailor sent word to Fenton that he'd be hunted down and hanged if he didn't return the goods. Fenton sent back the suit with a note: "I have returned your damned rags. In a short time I am going to burn your barns and houses and roast you all like a pack of kittens." And he did.

Fenton murdered a husband and wife in the course of one robbery conducted by the trio. The couple's daughter, though wounded, managed to escape and raise the alarm. Fagan and Burke had the sense to flee into the woods, while Fenton held up a wagon nearby and decided to drink up a bottle of brandy he found; he was shot while draining the bottle. Fagan and Burke were located later and also shot. Some citizens, outraged by missing out on helping to kill the notorious Fagan, dug up his body and hung it in chains from a tall tree so that the vultures could do their thing. When Fagan was reduced to a skeleton, the skeleton was cut down and the skull propped up at the base of the hanging tree. Since Fagan had been a pipe smoker, a pipe was placed in the jaws of the skull.

The ghosts of the threesome are said to haunt the backroads of the Pines, looking for more people to rob. Fagan's ghost is the one smoking a pipe.

The Bottomless "Blue Hole"

Why do some places feel more mysterious than others? What causes them to resonate a certain level of energy that parapsychologists term "supernatural"? Whatever the reasons, the myths and legends that have sprung up about such locations have been handed down to this day through the generations.

One such unique spot is the mysterious Blue Hole near the tiny town of Winslow, located off Piney Hollow Road near the Great Egg Harbor River. Not readily accessible, the Blue Hole still entices hikers and more serious researchers through the sand burrs, insects, and other natural barricades to its banks. The crystalline waters are frigid but completely clear because no vegetation apparently grows within the pool. It was named the Blue Hole because its transparent waters reflect the color of the sky. According to Kathryn H. Chalmers in *Down the Long-A-Coming*, chalybeate springs of medicinal value are located in the pool, which form a whirlpool at the center of the Hole and drain downward into the Atlantic Ocean. Scientists who have tried to measure the depth of the Blue Hole have apparently been stymied by the fact that their lines never seemed to reach the bottom, a fact that supported the "bottomless pit" theory.

Although the region has been populated since the mid-eighteenth century, no settlement has imposed upon the serenity that surrounds the Blue Hole, which continues to fascinate visitors because of its untamed quality. Chalmers noted that stories have been told of beautiful young women being drawn below the surface, where they live in "submarine splendor," and that young men have also reported being seized by unseen hands that tried to draw them down. A Native American tale says that the Blue Hole was born from the tears of a maiden crying over her faithless lover. But to this day, nothing has explained the presence of a crystal blue lake in a region best known for its tea-colored, cedar-fed waterways and nearby salty ocean.

Colonel Tom and the Captain

In the eighteenth century, tales of pirates' gold lured more than one foolish person into trouble, and Col. Tom Forrest proved to be no exception. The brash Philadelphia resident was frequently heard to boast that he knew where the infamous Blackbeard had buried his treasure. According to the colonel, it was somewhere between Elizabeth and Atlantic City, although he occasionally was heard to transfer the site of the loot to Fairmount Avenue in Philadelphia.

One day Forrest appeared in downtown Philadelphia waving an old parchment that he claimed revealed the secret location of the pirate's gold. Forrest claimed that the document was the last confession of a seaman who, before he was hanged, revealed that he and a number of others had helped Blackbeard bury a fortune in gold in the sands at Cooper's Point, across the Delaware River in New Jersey.

With most of his audience only too ready to believe him, Forrest quickly gathered a select few and invited them to assist him in locating the gold. They quickly agreed to divide the costs of the venture, and a few nights later, they crossed the Delaware River. Venturing out to Cooper's Point, the eager men were thrilled when someone's spade struck a metal surface below the ground not long after they started digging. But their excitement turned to fear when a pair of black-garbed men leaped from out of nowhere to block their way.

Forrest's companions fled in terror but were persuaded a short time later to return by their leader. Although every sound further frayed their nerves, the men continued to dig and soon unearthed a large metal pot that they carried back to their boat. They rowed it safely across the Delaware, but when they attempted to use some tackle to hoist the pot to the wharf, the equipment broke and the pot plunged into the river.

Everyone despaired of the lost treasure—except, it seemed, Col. Tom Forrest. Not long after the treasure hunt, Forrest seemed to enjoy a newfound prosperity that forced many of his former companions to take a fresh look at their leader. A number of them decided that the only way Forrest could have acquired his money was at their expense. They believed that he had probably emptied the pot before it left New Jersey and ultimately took him to court in an effort to recoup their share of the fortune in pirate's gold. Some say that a mysterious stranger still drops into waterfront bars in the vicinity and pays for his drinks with gold coins—which then disappear as the stranger departs.

The Hexed Town of Catawba

Southern New Jersey was once a thriving region, teeming with immigrants eager to work in the industries they found there. Iron-making, brickmaking, shipbuilding, and later, glassmaking were just some of the businesses that grew in the area, thanks to the endless acres of trees for fuel and for building, and the waterways that connected them to nearby cities. However, some of the entrepreneurs who invested in South Jersey were not all that successful. And some of them just might have been cursed.

According to William McMahon in *South Jersey Towns*, one town that mysteriously never made it—despite having all the right elements—was Catawba, located on the east side of the Great Egg Harbor River about four miles south of Mays Landing. "For years Catawba has been called a mystery village, and tales of strange deaths, hidden treasure, and such happenings" have clouded its history, he said. When he attempted to persuade one local man to help him find the town in the 1970s, McMahon was advised in no uncertain terms to stay away because "that place is hexed."

The story of Catawba began in the early nineteenth century, when George and Amy West of Burlington purchased two parcels of land on which to build their dream town. The first piece of ground was purchased in 1811 and the second in 1813. George, a prosperous merchant, laid out plans for the town and built a home for his family that was said to rival Joseph Bonaparte's elegant mansion in Bordentown. They added a Methodist church to the fledgling community, and shortly afterward, about twenty families settled there. For about twelve years, all seemed well. Catawba residents easily found employment in the shipbuilding trade in Mays Landing, and the little town thrived.

But then, on May 17, 1826, the West family experienced the first in a series of inexplicable deaths.

Fourteen-year-old Thomas Biddle West, the youngest member of the family, died less than two days after being taken ill. Three years later, James S. West, twenty-three, died on August 24 after a sudden illness. The father, George West, died the following month after suffering a similar attack. One week later, his wife, Amy, passed away under the same growingly suspicious circumstances. The only remaining survivors were two daughters, Charlotte Biddle West and Marie Inglis West, and the oldest son, Joseph.

For several years, speculation ran rampant that Joseph, in fact, had poisoned his parents and his younger brothers. Some felt that greed had motivated him to eliminate his parents and male siblings, who would have been in line to inherit their father's wealth. According to McMahon, "The surviving son sealed up all the graves, wrote flowery epitaphs, closed the mansion, and moved elsewhere."

Suspicion lingered, but it seemed the only crime Joseph was guilty of was being a bad businessman. Poor investments forced him to mortgage his father's dream home and later sell the entire property to pay off his debts. After a stint in jail for forgery, Joseph disappeared. Shortly afterward, the West mansion was demolished by its new owner, Gen. Enoch Doughty, one of the founders of the Camden and Atlantic Railroad. A practical man, Doughty needed lumber for some building he was doing in Absecon and tore down the house.

Rather than poison, it is possible that the Wests may have fallen victim to a plague that was transmitted by seamen who stopped in Mays Landing en route to the West Indies. The family, by all accounts, had regular contact with the sailors traveling through town.

Within a few short years, the population of Catawba dwindled to one—an unknown hermit who built a shelter on the West property. He spent his days digging holes in the ground but hid whenever strangers passed by. Before long, stories spread that he was searching for the West family's gold that supposedly had been buried there by Joseph, who never returned to claim his inheritance. Or had he? Three years after his arrival, the stranger disappeared as mysteriously as he had arrived—perhaps with his pockets lined with gold?

No evidence has ever been uncovered to determine what actually happened in the tiny Pinelands town almost two centuries ago. Today nothing remains of Catawba except the memory of a place where one family's dreams died, and the possibility of a hex lives on.

The White Stag of Shamong

Not every supernatural creature that has haunted the Pine Barrens over the years was malicious in nature. One story, recorded in verse by author W. Clement Moore, tells what happened to travelers one dark and stormy night, when they met the White Stag of Shamong:

Did you ever hear the story,
    Of the White Stag of Shamong?
Some say it's just a legend,
    But an interesting one.
Well, the old time stage drivers,
    Of early nineteenth century,
Claimed they often saw the White Stag,
    And he belongs in history.
One incident was oft related,
    About a dark and stormy night,

When a stage coach filled with travellers,
　　Were almost paralyzed with fright.

The wild wind blew, the thunder roared,
　　And the vivid lightning flashed,
Over treacherous roads, the stage coach tore,
　　As the rain against it splashed.
Then, as they neared Old Quaker Bridge,
　　A startled cry rang out!!
For blocking the road, the ghostly form,
　　Of the Great White Stag stood out.
Then, as suddenly as it came,
　　The White Stag disappeared,
While the driver and his passengers,
　　Sat petrified with fear.

At last, they decided to look around,
　　To see what lay ahead,
And sure enough, but for that Stag,
　　They all might have been dead.
For by the storm and raging wind,
　　The bridge had been torn away,
So the White Stag saved all their lives,
　　When he blocked the stage's way.
Listen! They say that Stag was seen
　　Again in nineteen fifty three,
Near the entrance to Old Quaker Bridge
　　Beside an old Pine Tree.

The Tale of Goody Garlick

During the seventeenth century, a number of women fell under suspicion of witchcraft in Europe and the American colonies. While the most famous cases were heard at the Salem Witch Trials in Massachusetts, others were held throughout different colonies by people who had left their homelands because of religious intolerance.

　　The victim of one such witch hunt was Elizabeth Garlick of East Hampton, Long Island. Wise in the use of herbs and other homemade medicines, "Goody" (an abbreviation of the term "Goodwife") Garlick soon found herself arrested and accused by friends and neighbors of poisoning a cow's milk, causing fever to a neighbor's child, and various other crimes that only a witch could commit. She was eventually brought to trial in Hartford, Connecticut, and was forced to endure repeated hearings in several courts. But her accusers were not able to bring sufficient evidence against her, and the court, which was reluctant to sentence her to death, finally set her free.

In 1691, she and her husband, John Parsons, fled to the wilds of Cape May County. There they lived in peaceful isolation for many years, raising their only child, Lydia, at the Leaming Plantation, today known as the small town of Rio Grande. There is no record that Elizabeth ever practiced herb lore or any other of her skills at her new home, perhaps due to her experiences in New England.

Strangely, her gravesite, to this day, remains unknown. Since it was common practice at that time to refuse burial in a Christian cemetery to anyone suspected of trafficking with the supernatural, did Goody Garlick continue to practice her arts? Were her New England neighbors' suspicions right all along? Although her burial place has never been found, some local residents say that around Halloween, a swirling white mist can be seen flowing through the wooded sections of Rio Grande where her daughter is buried.

The Jersey Witch Trials

More than four hundred newspapers flourished in Colonial America, carrying the news of the day. One popular publication was the *Pennsylvania Gazette*, which published, on October 22, 1730, an article describing a trial for witchcraft that had occurred recently in Mount Holly. The accused were subjected to a series of traditional trials to determine if they really were witches. Typically, a presumed witch was stripped naked (this helped draw a crowd, no doubt), shaved of body hair and carefully examined for a "devil's mark"—any scar or imperfection on the skin that resembled a mark of a cloven hoof. If no devil's mark was found, the examiners searched for a "witch's teat," from which the witch would suckle the devil. Any large mole could be judged a witch's teat. The accused were then weighed in scales balanced by a large Bible or collection of Bibles. Anyone who weighed more than God's Word (almost anyone would, of course) might be a witch.

In this case, the accused witches, a man and a woman, objected to undergoing the trials alone, countering that their righteous accusers should participate as well. A man and a woman agreed to represent the complainants, and a date was set for the trials.

Hundreds gathered to watch on that October day; it was an excuse for an outing for many of them. The first trial was the scales, which were hung expressly for the event from a gallows pole. As the prisoners and the crowd watched, a huge Bible belonging to the local justice was brought forward. According to the *Gazette*, "The Wizard was first put in the Scale, and over him was read a Chapter out of the Books of *Moses,* and then the Bible was put in the other Scale, (which being kept down before) was immediately let go; but to great Surprize of the Spectators, Flesh and Bones came down plump, and outweighed that great good Book by abundance." To the continued amazement of the crowd, the same thing happened to the next three participants, including the accusers.

The mob apparently was not satisfied with the results, however. It was decided that the trial by water would be a more accurate test, so the prisoners were escorted to the nearby millpond. The men and women were duly stripped, but for modesty's sake, the women were allowed to keep on their undergarments, then known as shifts. They were bound hand and foot and dropped into the water from the side of a barge. Each person, both accused and accuser, was tied around the waist with a rope, which was held by someone in the barge.

The newspaper gleefully reported:

> The Accuser Man being thin and spare, with some Difficulty began to sink at last; but the rest every one of them swam very light upon the Water. A Sailor in the [barge] jump'd out upon the Back of the Man accused, thinking to drive him down to the Bottom; but the Person bound, without any Help, came up some time before the other. The Woman Accuser, being told that she did not sink, would be duck'd a second Time; when she swam again as light as before. Upon which she declared, That she believed the Accused had bewitched her to make her so light, and that she would be duck'd again a Hundred Times, but she would duck the Devil out of her.

The accused man eventually admitted that he might be guilty of the charges against him. But the crowd felt that the women had an unfair advantage since their shifts probably helped them stay afloat. The disgruntled mob decided that it was only fair to hold the trial by water again when the weather was warm, with everyone completely naked.

Although this story maintained its hold on the public's imagination for centuries, it was later proven to be the work of Benjamin Franklin, a notorious prankster. Two sets of facts support the idea that Franklin simply made up the story to mock the idea of witch trials. It is known that as a boy, he wrote satirical letters to his brother's newspaper, signing them "Silence Dogood." An educated man, Franklin might have enjoyed making fun of witches and witch hunters. On the other hand, Ben Franklin is known to have hung around with members of England's notorious Hellfire Club when he represented Pennsylvania in London. Franklin was a close friend of Sir Francis Dashwood, who headed a Hellfire Club also called the Order of Saint Francis. They met on his country estate for heavy drinking, dalliances with prostitutes, perhaps a little drug abuse, and general mischief. The club's motto was "Do what you will" and emphasized individual choice and freedom from rules. Franklin was especially interested to learn that club members—who included members of Parliament and the government—also favored freedom for the American colonies. But the club had a dark side suggesting Satanism and devil worship, at least according to the enemies of the club members.

Was Ben Franklin's account of the Mount Holly witches intended to express a disbelief in witches or to ridicule, and thus undermine the authority of, witch hunters? In all fairness to Franklin, the lurid gossip about the Hellfire Club may have been greatly exaggerated by Sir Dashwood's political opponents. Historians today can't agree on whether the so-called Order of Saint Francis was a group of carousing, warlock wannabes who mostly got drunk together, a sort of eighteenth-century *Animal House* fraternity, or was seriously involved in devil worship. Benjamin Franklin himself said he was a deist—that is, he believed in God, but not in any particular organized religion. He contributed to Christ Church (Episcopal) and received a Christian burial in a Christian graveyard. Whatever Sir Dashwood's beliefs, it is more likely that Franklin was a skeptic concerning witches and witch hunters.

The Pirate Tree

In the nineteenth century, John Barber and Henry Howe coauthored a unique volume on New Jersey that included a variety of information, ranging from political commentary to geographic facts. Like many writers of the period, they were smart enough to spice their manuscript with lurid tales of the supernatural.

One such tale, according to Barber and Howe in *Historical Collections of the State of New Jersey,* involved the Pirate Tree, a large black walnut that once towered over Wood Street in Burlington. It was believed that no less a pirate than Blackbeard himself had buried gold and silver at the base of this tree. Although they normally traveled the eastern coast of New Jersey, the pirates supposedly came ashore one night, while a storm raged across the water, to secure their treasure at the Delaware River port. They covered the loot with a "broad, flat stone," but when Blackbeard demanded, "Who'll guard this wealth?" no one answered. Tradition demanded the ultimate sacrifice that none of the pirates were willing to pay.

Finally, one reckless outlaw, a Spaniard by birth, stepped forward and was shot by Blackbeard with a "charmed" bullet that would allow him to spring into action and fight off treasure hunters. He was buried upright and was apparently the right man for the job: Despite metal detectors and other modern innovations, no one to this day has ever publicly claimed the pirates' bounty. Some believers attest that the Spaniard had a companion buried with him—a large black dog, whose ghostly form has been seen wandering Wood Street late at night.

The Spaniard may have suffered a terrible fate, but his shipmates apparently didn't fare much better. It seems that the tree the pirates chose was a site where witches gathered, before the pirates usurped it for their own purposes. Witches met there one night to perform a ritual after the pirates intruded on their ceremony. It wasn't long after the sailors buried their gold and former shipmate and left that the witches returned to the tree and uttered a curse upon the intruders:

Away! Away! The night is foule, but fouler by far are ye!
The storm is fierce, but fiercer by far is your terrible destiny!

Your vessel shall sink amid mountain waves, and the fearful
  blasts of hell,
And you'll dwell for aye with the foule, foule fiend, whom here
  you have served so well!
Some shall go down with a bubbling groan on the ocean's
  pathless way,
Some shall be dashed on the flint rocks—the vulture and
  sea-bird's prey,
Some shall be washed alive on shore, to die on the gallows
  tree,
But gold, or wife, or children deare, none shall live ever to see.
Away, away, while the tempest howls, and the thunders are
  heard in wrath,
Away on your errand of guilt and blood, and destruction attend
  your path!

They cried the words in unison before flying away on their broomsticks, and by all accounts, the curse was successful. The pirate ship put out to sea a few days later, but it was never seen again.

It is said that a couple of men, made reckless by their greed, tried to dig up Blackbeard's gold not long after it was buried. They began shoveling one night, and instead of treasure, uncovered a hidden cavern where no less a villain than Blackbeard himself was hiding. Sprawled across his loot, his eyes burning with hate, the pirate glared up at the intruders, who quickly sprinted to safety, leaving their spades and lanterns behind. They shared their story with some trusted companions—no doubt over a pint or two of ale. But the next day, when the companions went to investigate their story, they discovered that there was not a mark around the base of the Pirate's Tree to show where they had dug.

A Trial by Witchcraft

No, not a trial *of* witchcraft, a trial *by* witchcraft. Or, if not witchcraft, then ancient superstition reaching back to the Saxon kings of England.

During the Middle Ages in Europe, there was a belief that the corpse of a murder victim would be seen to bleed, as though alive, at the touch of the murderer. This phenomenon, once wholeheartedly believed in, was used to decide the death penalty in those cases where the judge was reluctant to assign the death penalty in view of inconclusive or purely circumstantial evidence. The victim himself or herself would condemn the murderer, absolving the judge of this responsibility.

A famous trial was held in Salem in 1692, in which an accused murderer was condemned by the corpse of the victim. The case was Rex et Regina (King William and Queen Mary) vs. Lutherland, and the legal principle involved was the Law of the Bier. The bier is the furniture that supports the dead body on display. One Thomas Lutherland, a carpenter, was accused of murdering John Clark, a merchant, and stealing his goods.

Lutherland claimed that he was innocent; that he had paid Clark for the goods found in his possession, and that he had not touched the merchant. When the jurors, undecided among themselves, suggested that he be judged by the Law of the Bier, the accused agreed. The rotting corpse of John Clark was brought to the courtroom. Thomas Lutherland touched it, very reluctantly, immediately withdrawing his hand and bursting into convulsions. The corpse did not bleed, the record says, but Lutherland became hysterical and confessed on the spot. The sight and touch of the decaying body of his victim convinced him that he should pay the ultimate penalty. Thomas Lutherland was hanged after signing a full confession.

Locals claim that Lutherland's ghost can be seen, in the shadows of dusk, kneeling on the banks of the river, vainly trying to wash off the taint of touching his victim's body.

Jersey Lightning and the Clever Indian

Old-timers living near Rancocus Creek in Burlington County recall a ghost that appeared there only on the coldest days in the dead of winter. An old Indian, clad in traditional garb, could be seen wandering along the backroads or on the banks of the creek itself. Oddly, he carefully carried a large, handmade basket, which the figure would bring up to his lips and drink from, as though the basket were a mug.

This unusual, and seldom seen, ghost has a story behind it. A story of how a clever Indian outsmarted a local farmer who was famous for his homemade hard apple cider, known as "Jersey lightning." Jersey lightning was famous in early America. It was a product of three well-known facts: Apples grow plentifully in New Jersey; New Jerseyans (and their neighbors) appreciate a drink or two on occasion; and not only is it easy to make hard cider, but it also travels well and more than repays the cost of delivering it to nearby cities.

It was the 1740s. Ashatama was one of the last full-blooded Lenni-Lenape in the neighborhood. He wove beautiful baskets from local reeds and willow trees, trading them for whatever he needed. Ashatama approached one local man, who enjoyed a good reputation for the quality and potency of his "jack." The distilling was easy. He placed a barrel of fermenting applejack on a back porch in winter. Every day, he'd lift off the lid and take out the disk of ice atop the cider, thus disposing of the water and concentrating the alcohol, which didn't freeze, in the barrel. Over a winter, the intense cold would produce a beverage to "keep out the cold."

Ashatama wished to trade his baskets for hard cider. However, the Colonial legislature had passed a law forbidding the colonists to supply alcohol to Indians. Native Americans could not metabolize alcohol as quickly as Europeans. It was a genetic thing—Indians got a lot drunker a lot faster than whites.

So the Jersey lightning maker refused Ashatama's request for his product. The Indian persisted. The hard cider man proposed a deal: He would give Ashatama all the drink that his basket would hold. "Even a big basket?" asked the Indian. Even a big basket—but, added the farmer, no fair caulking the basket with pitch. No pitch, agreed Ashatama. The Indian departed, and the farmer's dilemma left with him, or so he thought.

One cold winter day, Ashatama was seen repeatedly dipping his biggest basket into the ice-chocked Rancocus Creek near the farmer's house. The Indian presented his basket, now lined with ice, to be filled with the "good stuff." "No pitch," said Ashatama. The farmer had to laugh at how neatly he'd been outsmarted; he filled the frozen and thus leak-proof basket. Ashatama went his merry, increasingly inebriated way.

Close observation of Ashatama's ghost, with his ice-lined basket, will reveal a certain unsteadiness of walk. Jersey lightning is a potent treat, enjoyed every winter by Ashatama's ghost.

The Patriotic Ghosts of Hancock House

That there are a lot of ghosts at the old Hancock House is beyond doubt, at least to believers in ghosts. Just how many ghosts depends on just how many patriots were cruelly massacred there shortly before dawn on March 21, 1778. Different sources say thirty, sixty, or even ninety. By any estimate, the massacre produced many anguished, restless souls.

It is easy to forget that not all Colonial Americans were patriots. A number of citizens remained loyal to King George; know as Tories, they spied on their Revolutionary neighbors, served as scouts or informants for British forces, and even served in the British armies, oppressing their patriotic friends and relatives. It has been said that an army marches on its belly; soldiers need food and their horses need food. In many wars, before and after the American Revolution, armies on both sides organized foraging parties to go out into the countryside and gather—steal—food and supplies. British troops stationed in Philadelphia during the cold winter of 1777–78 were running low on food. It was decided to send soldiers into nearby New Jersey to find grain and livestock. The British especially enjoyed a good roast beef dinner, even tastier when robbed from a patriot's farm.

As the British marched through South Jersey, they naturally stuck to the few established roads, which necessarily converged on the very few stone bridges across the tidal tributaries of the Delaware. Bridges thus were strategic points in military strategy.

And so it came about that Hancock's Bridge in Salem County was the objective of a mixed force of British and Tory soldiers numbering about fifteen hundred. They had just fought an inconclusive battle with American troops at nearby Quinton Bridge and hoped to decisively defeat the Jersey militia at Hancock's Bridge. But the main body of Jerseymen had moved on, leaving a small guard to defend the bridge.

Approaching the bridge stealthily by night, the British were frustrated to find that the four hundred-strong American force they expected to encounter had already withdrawn, leaving a small rear guard who were bunked in Judge Hancock's handsome stone house by the bridge. The British bayoneted the sentries, broke into the house, and silently slit the throats of the helpless, sleeping Americans. In the confusion and darkness, they also murdered Judge Hancock, a Tory who had been taken prisoner in his own house.

This dishonorable, cowardly massacre added many converted Tories to the American cause. It also added to New Jersey's ghost population. It is said that the ghosts of the American victims, having learned their lesson, now rest by day and patrol vigilantly at night. If you are challenged by ghostly soldiers at Hancock's Bridge, the correct reply to the challenge "Who goes there?" is "A true blue American!" Patriot soldiers, you see, wore uniforms of dark blue and white, in contrast to the British redcoats.

The Haunted Schoolteacher

Teaching was a difficult profession in the early nineteenth century. Although standards were much less strict in those days, teachers were underpaid then as now, and they were also expected to handle the responsibility of teaching different grade levels at the same time in a one-room schoolhouse. Since there were few requirements for the job in those days—usually just an eighth-grade education—the profession sometimes attracted decidedly eccentric personalities.

One such teacher was Cadchi Ayars, who taught district school in Salem County. Harold F. Wilson, documented her story in *The Jersey Shore:*

> [Cadchi Ayars claimed] she was bothered by a ghost which groaned. A former student wrote later that people came in crowds to hear the ghost groan. Horses and carriages were tied up all along the fence by the schoolhouse. First Cadchi would get the class repeating their lessons out loud and then the ghost would perform. This went on for weeks. The children were so frightened that it was no trouble for their parents to keep them home nights. Finally a bright young lawyer from Salem discovered the source of the moan, which could be heard only when all the pupils were reciting. The noise, he found, emanated from the throat of the teacher. She was dismissed and the school closed for a while."

The World's Largest Ghost

Although no one knows for sure which of New Jersey's three Greenwiches is the actual town, legend has it that the "world's largest woman," Catherine Learch, was probably born in Salem County's Greenwich in 1816. When her unfortunate mother died in childbirth, Catherine's father began to bottle-feed her with a secret formula. The child apparently thrived on the ingredients—by the time she reached adulthood, her weight was reported to be 760 pounds, with a waist that measured 9 feet, 6 inches.

By all accounts, the young woman's size was not a deterrent to a happy life. She reportedly married William Schooley and eventually moved to Ohio. From there, the couple traveled throughout the United States, amazing everyone with her physical presence and her life story. In death, her obese ghost apparently returned to her hometown, where she wanders along the main street at night, looking for a little snack. But, don't worry—the ghost waddles along so slowly that you can easily outrun it.

The Confederate Ghosts of Finn's Point

Defending Philadelphia against potential attack by warships sailing up the Delaware River has been a military concern from the Revolution to World War II. Finn's Point, named for the early Finnish settlers imported by the New Sweden Colony, was the site of an early Swedish fort and, after 1837, a Federal gun battery. This Finn's Point Battery complemented the larger and more powerful Fort Delaware, built on Pea Patch Island in the middle of the river; the crossfire between the Jersey shore and the island would doom any enemy ships.

Fort Delaware was built of solid brick and equipped with powerful guns by the start of the Civil War. It never fired a shot, though, as the Confederate Navy was far too weak to go on the offensive against Northern ports. The fort became, instead, a high-security prison for Confederate prisoners of war.

As a military prison, Fort Delaware earned a truly grim reputation as a deathtrap. It became infamous as a Union counterpart of

the Confederacy's notorious Andersonville Prison in Georgia. Built atop many pilings on a swampy island just barely above high tide, Fort Delaware's only water supply was contaminated river water. The heavily overcrowded prisoners suffered greatly from lack of medical care, malnutrition, mosquito-borne malaria, festering infections, and dysentery, at the time, a fatal disease.

Soon daily boatloads of corpses were docking at Finn's Point, where the dead were unceremoniously dumped into long trenches. More than twenty-seven hundred Confederates died of filth and neglect. Their mostly unmarked graves are testimony to the bitterness of the Civil War. It is said that President Lincoln, though painfully aware of the horrendous death rates in both Union and Confederate prison camps, refused to authorize large-scale exchanges of prisoners of war. His overriding goal was to win the war, and he reasoned that the South would benefit more from such exchanges than the North, which had the advantage of a much larger population.

It is said that the justifiably angry Confederates are restless and vengeful ghosts who now haunt Finn's Point and adjacent Fort Mott. Visitors report hearing the faint, poignant notes of taps being played at dusk on foggy, moonless nights. Shadowy ranks of soldiers marching in formation are seen on occasion. One family, out for an evening drive at dusk near the Confederate gravesites, experienced a frightening car problem. Their new car suddenly stopped dead. The engine would not turn over, and none of the lights would work. They abandoned the car for the night, amidst a chorus of moans and shouts from the adjacent graveyard. Prominent on the car's hood were the shiny chrome letters that spelled out "L-I-N-C-O-L-N."

The Ghost Doctor Who Made House Calls

If it's unusual for doctors to make house calls these days, how much more rare would be a doctor who apparently made house calls for decades after his death. But then, there was nothing common about James Still, the famed "Black Doctor of the Pines," either in his life or after his death.

James Still was born in 1812 at Indian Mills, the site of America's first Indian reservation. His parents were freed slaves. They had chosen this isolated little community in the Pinelands to escape the almost constant harassment of proving that they were legally free and not runaway slaves. His father had, in fact, bought his and his wife's freedom, by working extra hard and saving up money, so the Still family was distinguished by an impressive work ethic. Their neighbors were a mix of African-Americans and Native Americans who'd stayed behind when the reservation, founded in 1758, was sold off as most Indian residents decided to move to New York State in 1801.

The poor of Indian Mills couldn't afford to go to doctors; they doctored themselves with herbal remedies. Their knowledge of the healing properties of plants came from Native American traditions, augmented by African and European folk medicine.

James Still decided that he would become a doctor. One problem was that formal education was not accessible to a poor black boy, at least not beyond a few months of introduction to reading, writing, and arithmetic. Still's knowledge of herbal cures and folk medicine became encyclopedic. He was far ahead of his time in recognizing the real benefits of alternative medicines and had an open mind to ancient folk wisdom in healing.

Soon his herbs and medicines were earning him a reputation as a great healer. He bought a carriage with money earned by manufacturing herbal medicines for a Philadelphia pharmacist and began traveling the roads around Indian Mills and Medford, treating people of all races from his box of "nature's cures." When challenged by the jealous medical establishment, Still was able to defend himself. He had never claimed to be a doctor; people honored him with that title when his cures worked. There was nothing illegal about selling herbs to people who wished to buy them. His carriage kept rolling down the highways as he delivered his "prescriptions" in person.

After his death, probably from a stroke brought on by overwork, his onetime patients and friends became aware of his continuing care. It seems that death didn't erase the good doctor's concern for his patients. People began finding little bundles of herbs, neatly tied with string, on their doorsteps in the morning. Not coincidentally, these herbs would be the same that Dr. Still had prescribed for their ailments while he was alive. Apparently the doctor was continuing his care from beyond the grave. Some former patients swore that the night before the herbs appeared on their doorsteps, they heard the clip-clop, clip-clop of a horse-drawn carriage moving down the street. The ghost of Dr. Still was continuing to perform his life's ambition of healing.

Fiddling with the Devil

Legends have always followed gifted musicians, some of whom reportedly were willing to "sell their souls" for the opportunity to play the perfect song or sing the perfect note. Others have allegedly challenged the Devil in musical contests in order to save their souls—or possibly just to satisfy their egos and prove they were more talented than the Prince of Darkness.

One such fiddler, renowned throughout the Pinelands for his playing, was Sammy Giberson, or Sammy Buck, who was repeatedly heard to declare he could outplay the Devil himself. It was unlikely that Sammy ever expected anyone to accept his challenge. Still, he was not too surprised when, on his way home from a local dance one night, he was confronted at a bridge by a tall, dark stranger who proved to be none other than Satan himself.

Residents of the Pinelands still delight in telling of the duel between Sammy and the Devil, as they drew their bows and began to play. For every song that Satan selected, Sammy offered an equally difficult tune, until finally, he began a song so sweet, so mournful, and so intricate that the Devil was unable to continue. Fortunately for Sammy, Old Nick was so moved by the music that he was a gracious loser. And Sammy Giberson continued on his way home, knowing that he had not boasted about his talent in vain. According to David Cohen in *The Folklore and Folklife of New Jersey,* "This motif of 'beating the devil' can be traced back to European folklore. Similar stories have been told about the Italian violinist Niccolo Paganini (1782–1840) and the Norwegian violinist Ole Bull (1810–1880)." Although there are versions in which Sammy loses and forfeits his soul, most people who relate the tale prefer to have him finish as the winner.

The Wizard of Hanover Furnace

Jerry Munyhon (also spelled Munyhun, Munglun, or Monehan) was known as the Wizard of Hanover Furnace, who had willingly sold his soul to the Devil in exchange for magical powers. According to William McMahon in *South Jersey Towns,* he was said to cause trees to "chop themselves down." He also had a magical walking stick that ran errands for him.

Munyhon, who reportedly lived between Brindletown and Hanover Furnace in the late eighteenth century, was notorious for casting spells over anyone he didn't like. One story told by Pinelands residents recounts how Munyhon exacted his revenge when the Jones family, his employers at Hanover Furnace, refused to pay him. The wizard disappeared from the site for a few days, and when he returned, he discovered that the furnace was closed down because the fires weren't burning. Munyhon offered to fix the problem if his employers paid him. When they accepted his offer, a flock of white crows streamed from the chimneys—birds that some say Munyhon had "witched" there in the first place.

Another day, when his employers refused to pay him, Munyhon reportedly cast a spell that sent their team of horses into a nearby pond. When he offered to get them out for a price, the Joneses agreed. A few minutes later, they found their animals tied to a hitching post. His powers reportedly included the ability to entice cows into a swamp and to turn clamshells into dollars (which later returned to their original form).

On the night he died, the story goes, there was a knock on his front door at midnight. Munyhon, who had not been feeling well for a few days, asked his wife to see who was at the door. When she opened it, there was a man standing there. He asked for her husband. After his wife relayed the stranger's request, Munyhon sighed and said, "It's the Devil. Tell him I'm ready." With those words, he died. However, some local residents will swear, whenever any mischief seems to be at work, that the spirit of Jerry Munyhon still lingers, reluctant to leave the woods for a much less pleasant alternative.

The Mount Holly Jail

Burlington County Prison, also known as the Mount Holly Jail, is one of the oldest jails in New Jersey, if not *the* oldest. Erected in 1808, the imposing gray stone building served as home to countless prisoners through the years. Some, however, apparently were not freed from the jail even after death. The story is that if you stop by Cell 5 on the third floor at night, you may hear Joseph Clough rattling the chains that once bound him there. Clough, convicted of murdering his mistress with a table leg, was a prisoner on death row until he was hanged in the 1850s. Others have reported the sound of gates opening and the echoes of feet tramping down dank corridors. Few are brave enough to spend much time in the menacing environment after dark, when the spirits begin to move.

The jail was designed by architect Robert Mills, a friend of Thomas Jefferson, who later designed the Washington Monument and part of Independence Hall. It was considered a radical departure from existing prisons because, like modern jails, it was designed to promote rehabilitation rather than punishment. The prison, which remained in use until 1966, was later restored as a museum and today is operated by the Burlington County Prison Museum Association.

Bessie's Coming-Out Party

Some longtime residents of Cape May claim to have occasionally seen a shimmering, pale figure of a beautiful young woman strolling along the seafront very late at night on early summer evenings. She appears to be radiantly happy, and so she should be, for she has been reliving a happy occasion: She was just the star of an old-fashioned coming-out party. Early in the twentieth century, these lavish dinner-dances were customarily held to formally introduce young women to society as young adults now eligible for dating.

Bessie Warfield, as she was called in childhood (her real first name was a family name, and not particularly feminine), grew up as a boardinghouse cook's daughter. She early determined that someday she would live like a princess in a fairy tale. Her hometown was Baltimore, and in keeping with long-established tradition dating from before the Civil War, Cape May was the preferred seaside retreat of Baltimoreans with social pretensions. And pretension is the key word, as the slender, rather boyish-looking, newly adult "member of society" had little going for her besides a driving ambition. As a small child, she had undergone an embarrassing, even humiliating, move from a luxurious home to a run-down boardinghouse. Her mother, daughter of a socially prominent family, had gone from riches to rags following the untimely death of her wealthy husband.

Why does Bessie's ghost wander happily along Cape May's seafront when later life saw her living mostly in France and New York City? Perhaps, in the afterglow of her first grown-up and evidently successful party, Cape May was the last time she experienced innocent joy at life's prospects before her. This Baltimore girl, whose coming-out party on Cape May's seafront drive was no doubt scrimped and saved for for months, was to achieve both fame and notoriety following her third marriage. She was the woman for whom a king gave up his throne; many admired and envied her, but many others hated her. Her real name? Wallis Warfield Spenser Simpson Windsor, a.k.a. the Duchess of Windsor.

Runnemede's Restless Spirit

Settled in the seventeenth century, Runnemede has a long and colorful history that includes one of its most prominent geographical features, Irish Hill. Also known as Iris Hill, Irish Hill rises 146 feet above sea level, and deposits dating to about sixty-five million years ago are evidence that glaciers once moved across this portion of New Jersey. The hill has been the site of a variety of local legends, including one that Gen. George Washington fought British troops there. Apparently the story grew around the remains of trenches that can be seen in the hillside. Another tale recounts that highwaymen used to rob stagecoaches as they crossed the hill, but local historians disproved that theory when they discovered that by the time stagecoaches ran through the area, the road over Irish Hill was no longer in use.

Local residents also recount the sad story of Aaron Van Dexter. The Great Depression crushed the hopes and dreams of many people throughout the country. In Runnemede, it claimed the life of Aaron Van Dexter, who had dreamed of reaping great rewards after he invested in the Peters place, an old farm located on the south side of Smith's Lane. In 1927, Van Dexter decided to gamble on creating a housing development on part of his land. A real estate developer offered him $5,000 for the option to build, and before long, the borough had put in sidewalks, curbs, and gutters in anticipation of the project. However, the Depression hit before any lots could be sold, and Van Dexter was confronted by the specter of increased property taxes and improvement assessments. With only $5,000 available, he knew he would never be able to pay the bills, so one night, he went out to the barn and hanged himself from the rafters. The Peters place was eventually torn down to make way for an influx of houses. But some nights, the locals say, you can see a figure walking slowly toward the place where the barn once stood, reluctantly preparing to meet his fate.

Some Ghosts of Gloucester County

Virginia Joslin, a famed ghost hunter and expert on hauntings, believes that the vicinity of Mullica Hill in Gloucester County, is a hot spot (or, in witnesses' reports, literally a "cold spot") for hauntings and ghostly manifestations. *Ghosts of Gloucester County,* a survey of Gloucester County ghosts that Joslin edited, recounts the most famous ghost stories of the area.

Mullica Hill's old Ashcroft place is a gray stucco house distinguished by five separate cellars, the products of extensive rebuilding and expansion over the years. New owners first noticed that their puppy, normally friendly and playful, became agitated and aggressive when in one cellar. At odd hours, doors would slam and heavy footsteps were heard—when there was no one else in the house. The residents started using the heavy iron bolts that a previous owner had installed, interestingly, on both sides of all interior doors. Whether bolted or not, the slamming sounds continued—but the bolts remained undisturbed.

In Thorofare, a small Cape Cod house off Delaware Street has had a unique history of exploding teeth. When the baby teeth of children are left under the pillow for the tooth fairy, they are found fragmented almost into powder. Not typical tooth fairy behavior. One tooth left out on a table exploded in front of witnesses. Nearby, on Crown Point Road, rooms in an old house would suddenly appear to be brilliantly lit at night—but there were no lamps of any kind, and this happened on moonless nights.

In Wenonah, in a house about seventy years old at the time, window shades suddenly have gone up or down or fell off the window entirely. A medicine cabinet routinely emptied itself. Clothes fell off hangers in the closets. Sometimes, a tall man in an overcoat was seen briefly when no one should be there.

The Otto House on the south end of Mickleton on the Old Kings Highway, built of brown Jersey sandstone, once belonged to a surgeon with George Washington's army. On returning home at night, the owners observed a flickering light in an upstairs room. No one should have been in the house. As their car entered the driveway, the headlights and engine both shut off by themselves. When local police, summoned to investigate this possible break-in, entered the mysteriously lit room, their flashlights suddenly went dark and could not be turned on again. No trace of an intruder was found.

At Gibbstown's Brown House, pots and pans tumbled to the floor, apparently by themselves. At times, sounds of a large, joyous party were heard in the basement—but no one was there. The current residents occasionally saw a woman dressed all in white, in 1920s vintage clothing.

Glassboro has at least three different ghosts. The best-known ghost haunted an old house on Main Street. The figure of a little girl, about age eight, appeared in an upper-floor bedroom. Thudding sounds were heard on the stairs, as though someone was falling down those stairs. The ghostly face of a small girl sometimes stared out at passers-by from an upstairs window.

The story is that more than a hundred years ago, a small girl died as a result of falling down those stairs. There are two versions of the story. Either children were wrestling at the top of the stairs and the fall was an accident, or the girl's uncle pushed her. The girl's name was Elizabeth, but she was called Lizzy by the many temporary residents who have reportedly seen her. She sometimes has knelt on the back of sleeping students (the house has had no permanent residents for decades; college students rent rooms but seldom stay very long) and whispered unintelligibly into their ears. A spiritualist called in to investigate the haunting claimed that the girl was strangled, then thrown down the stairs. Possibly her uncle had been abusing her.

Rowan University's campus in Glassboro had a haunted building, frequented by at least one, or possibly two, ghosts. Bunce Hall, the university's oldest and original classroom building, was said to have ghosts. Both alleged ghosts seemed to be benign and more interested in checking on progress at Rowan than in harassing the living. The more frequently seen ghost was that of a former professor, Elizabeth Tohill, for whom the building's auditorium was named. Tohill taught at Rowan, then Glassboro State College, for twenty-six years, between 1930 and 1956. She served as director of dramatic arts, directing student plays and teaching drama. She never married, focusing her whole life on her teaching and directorial duties. Professor Tohill's ghost was said to have appeared backstage during both rehearsals and performances of her favorite plays. Once she was said to have joined the chorus line during a musical performance. A videotape of the show showed an extra, unidentified dancer in the back row.

Less frequent appearances were made by the ghost of Thomas Whitney, the wealthy glass manufacturer whose estate became the university's campus in the early 1920s. His Victorian brownstone mansion, Holly Bush, served as the college president's home and was the site of a 1967 summit conference between President Lyndon Johnson and Soviet Premier Aleksey Kosygin. The Whitney ghost was that of a tall, distinguished gentleman dressed in Victorian splendor, who strolled around the campus in early evenings, supposedly shaking his head disapprovingly at any changes in his beloved onetime estate. His ghost must be pretty unhappy, as the university is growing quickly and change is ongoing.

The Wreck of the Blue Comet

Travel through Chatsworth on a warm summer night and you just might catch an echo of a tragedy that occurred near that small town on August 19, 1939. Some say that the ghosts of the hapless passengers who rode the Blue Comet that day still haunt the site where the luxury train derailed, resulting in the deaths of almost everyone on board.

The Blue Comet was a specialty train that traveled from Jersey City down through the Pine Barrens. Owned and operated by the Central Railroad of New Jersey, the train made two round-trips every day in less than three hours. It made one stop in Hammonton to pick up additional passengers before continuing on to Atlantic City.

The Blue Comet was blue inside and out. The cars and the sleek diesel engines were blue, as were the seats, carpeting, and table linens. The men who worked the line wore blue uniforms, and the tickets purchased for the ride were also blue.

It was an immediately popular ride after it first started its run on February 21, 1929. At that time, Atlantic City had experienced another renaissance, and gambling, liquor, and sex were available almost anywhere in that wide-open town. For ten years, the train carried passengers back and forth from North Jersey to the Queen of Resorts, until that fateful day in August when the rains began to fall.

For many weeks, South Jersey had been experiencing a serious drought. But on August 19, the sky turned overcast and released a torrential downpour that government weather stations later recorded as more than eight inches of rain falling within a few hours. Water flooded the rail line, and when the Blue Comet hit the stretch near Chatsworth, it canted off the tracks. Brakes squealed and passengers screamed as the train slid to a stop. Local residents described the crash as horrendous, and hundreds were killed in the wreck.

Today the rusting remains of the train still lie scattered along the abandoned stretch of track, which went out of use a few years later. If you listen closely, however, you might still hear the blast of the air horn that once resounded through the Pine Barrens, letting area residents know that the Blue Comet was flying by—on its final, fatal run.

A Gentle Spirit

Like many rural South Jersey communities, Landisville was once filled with small, thriving farms that produced everything from squash and eggplant to peppers and tomatoes, and then some. What the families did not eat themselves, they sold at the local farmers' market to restaurants and produce companies. The residents of the town took pride in their farms, which were partly responsible for New Jersey's nickname of the Garden State.

Aunt Angie was the matriarch of one local family. In her younger days, she had spent her days plowing and planting, working side by side with her husband and children to create a home and a profitable farm. When she died in 1965 at the age of eighty-seven, she left behind several hundred acres of prime land and a rambling farmhouse filled with as many memories as heirlooms. At least, the family thought she had left it . . . at first.

It seemed that Aunt Angie had derived so much joy out of life, although hers was not an easy one, that she decided not to leave the family home. While most paranormal researchers agree that a spirit usually lingers only when its body has suffered a violent death, she seemed to be the exception to the rule. Angie's niece, Victoria, recalled her first encounter with the kindly ghost:

> John and I had just gotten married in 1968, and my mother, Angie's sister, said we should live at the farmhouse for a while to save money before we bought our own place. I loved the idea because I had always visited Aunt Angie there and I had wonderful memories of the place. Well, we moved in and we hadn't even been there a month before some strange things started to happen.
>
> Although my mother had packed most of Aunt Angie's things after she died, we had a couple of knickknacks of hers still out in our living room. One afternoon, I had rearranged the pieces on a bookshelf, but before I could finish, I was interrupted by a telephone call. I went into the kitchen to answer the phone, and when I returned a few minutes later, the pieces had been moved back to their original positions. For a minute, I thought my husband had come home and was playing a joke on me. But then, I realized that the pieces were back the way Aunt Angie always kept them.
>
> It gave me a chill, but with everything else that was going on at the time, I really didn't think any more about it. However, that seemed to be just the beginning. We began to hear footsteps late at night in the bedroom where Aunt Angie had slept. Occasionally, I would smell her perfume in the upstairs hall. Small objects continued to be moved around. Finally, as I walked into my kitchen one night, I could smell bread baking. As I turned the corner, I saw my aunt bending over the oven, as though preparing to take the loaves out, just as she had done a million times before. I went weak in the knees. She looked up, smiled at me, and immediately disappeared.

Although Victoria loved her aunt and did not feel threatened by her, after a few more months, she asked her husband if he would mind moving out a little ahead of schedule. In her words, it was just "too creepy" to be seeing someone in your house when you knew they were buried just a few miles away. "My mother was a little upset when she heard we were moving," she said. "It turns out, she knew all along that her sister's spirit was still in the house. She never said anything because, to her, it didn't matter. After all, it was just family."

Since the young couple moved, a number of different people have rented the property, but no one has reported anything strange over the past thirty years. However, according to Victoria, her niece is getting married soon, and when she does, the newlyweds plan to move into what the family still calls "Aunt Angie's house." Although Victoria made a point of telling her niece about the ghost of her great-aunt, the young woman laughed off the whole idea. But when they do move in, Victoria has no doubt that they will be visited by the kind-hearted spirit who apparently lives there. After all, family is family.

Down the Shore

ASK ANY BEACHGOER ABOUT THE JERSEY SHORE, AND IT'S UNLIKELY THAT he or she will talk about anything except the sandy beaches, the ocean waves, and the number of people who flock there each summer. The happy resort image of New Jersey's seashore is in sharp contrast to its place in the spirit world. Sun-filled days of innocent fun in this realm of sand and surf are the tourists' view of the shore. But the 127-mile-long string of beaches has a dark side—a shadowy world of greed, violent death, betrayal, and murder—with a number of tragic shipwrecks, the murderous actions of wreckers who lured ships into dangerously shallow waters, and many visits by ruthless pirates to these shores.

Was it an omen that the first two explorers to see the Jersey shore—Giovanni da Verrazano and Henry Hudson—had very bad luck afterward? Da Verrazano was the first European known to have viewed the Jersey beaches—from a distance. Rather than attempting to land here, he sailed along the coast in 1524 and claimed the area for his employers, the French. They took no practical steps to claim this, to them, unimpressive region. Da Verrazano was later captured, killed, and eaten by cannibals in the Caribbean.

It wasn't until 1609—eighty-five years later—that another explorer, Henry Hudson, bothered to sail along New Jersey's shores. Like Verrazano, Hudson was not especially excited about the seashore and didn't get off the boat to look at it. Later, while exploring Hudson Bay in Canada, his boat was locked in ice over the winter. His crew mutinied and set him adrift in a small boat come spring, while they sailed for home. Hudson was never seen or heard from again.

Few now are aware of the first impressions of the early explorers, who saw little good and much to fear as they surveyed the coast between the Hudson and Delaware Rivers. Henry Hudson noted that the waves broke over shallow, submerged sandbars many yards off the beaches, and that the inlets or channels between the islands along the southern shores were narrow, twisting, and only a few feet deep—not a welcoming shoreline for sailors. Like other seafarers before and since, Hudson was favorably impressed not with New Jersey's coast, but by the great natural harbors that flanked it to the north and south. The broad, sandy beaches sloping gently into the waves allow vacationers to wade out into the surf for the thrill of braving the breakers. But the very same qualities that make New Jersey's ocean shoreline a great natural playground also made it, for centuries, a deathtrap. Very shallow water, breaking waves, and the low, flat horizon of most of the seashore made this a hostile shoreline for early sailors. Except, that is, for those who flew the skull and crossbones.

This graveyard of the Atlantic, as it became known to early seafarers, has become as haunted as other graveyards. No one really knows how many victims of shipwrecks lie restlessly on the seabed, their bones tossed about like seashells by waves and currents, their spirits condemned to wander the sands.

Shipwrecks

Because of the great number of shipwrecks along the New Jersey shorelines, some of the first, tallest, and most famous lighthouses in the country are found here. And the very first federal government-sponsored lifesaving stations were built along the Jersey shore. Sandy Hook Light is the oldest lighthouse in the United States. Built in 1764, it was intended to guide ships safely into New York Harbor and was financed by contributions from New York merchants. During the Revolution, American patriots tried unsuccessfully to tear it down. Now that the light was guiding

British warships to safe waters, the Americans wanted more shipwrecks, not fewer. It is claimed that this lighthouse, like many others, is haunted.

The scene of so many shipwrecks, Sandy Hook has its share of notable ghosts, some of which haunt not only the lighthouse, but also the ruins of Fort Hancock. The notorious Whitlock-Seabrook House in old Port Monmouth is a kind of state capital for ghosts. This 1663 house, also known as the Spy House, is alleged to be home to as many as thirty different ghosts—a New Jersey record.

Was the dreadful loss of life, and the resultant hauntings of the beaches, the motive for the establishment of a chain of federal lifesaving stations along the Jersey shore? Many people thought so at the time. The restless spirits of drowned sailors and ships' passengers have haunted virtually every seaside community. It is said that ghosts are particularly active when they are not resigned to their fate, when their deaths were not the result of true accidents but were caused by criminals. Two varieties of mass murderers have visited New Jersey beaches in times past: wreckers and pirates.

Wreckers, sometimes also called pirates, caused many shipwreck disasters along the coast by luring ships onto the sandbars and beaches in order to loot their cargoes and strip dead bodies of valuables. It started innocently enough. People living near the then-isolated beaches were in the habit of beachcombing for anything useful that might wash up on their doorsteps. Shipwrecks were a bonanza for beachcombers. Abandoned cargoes were salvaged and often sold at auction. "Finders, keepers" was the rule. Many a ship's timbers were used to build houses, furniture, or fences ashore.

There was nothing wrong with recycling these gifts of the sea, even though they were the products of natural disasters. The problem came when a few locals, lured by the prospects of easy pickings, decided to not only take advantage of shipwrecks, but to cause them. In the days before most lighthouses had been built, ships cruising along the coast had few clues as to exactly where the shoreline was at night. It was a very low-profile shore, with few houses or landmarks. On moonless or stormy nights, wreckers would tie a lantern to a donkey's tail and lead the animal slowly along the beach. The light, swinging slightly from the creature's tail and making slow progress parallel to the shipping lanes, was a good imitation of a ship's riding light, swinging back and forth with the sway of a ship under sail. Ships at sea, seeing the light of what appeared to be another ship, would misjudge the actual distance to the shore and thus venture into shallow waters and be grounded on the sands. Unable to free themselves or maneuver, the ships were pounded by the surf and broke up. Cargo, sailors, and passengers alike spilled into the sea. Many lives were sacrificed to the greed of the wreckers, who were also called "mooncussers" (moon cursers), as they were said to have "cussed" a full moon, which helped navigators avoid danger. The wreckers were much more interested in salvaging cargo than in rescuing people. The dead who washed ashore were stripped of jewelry, money, and even clothing, then left unburied.

Pirates and Their Treasures

Pirates. The word sent shivers through the civilized world between the seventeenth and nineteenth centuries. The merciless buccaneers terrorized sailing ships and coastal towns, and they frequented the Jersey shore because it offered numerous opportunities. Here was a lonely coast with few to notice or report the presence of unfamiliar ships or sailors. The coast was close to busy ports, with many valuable cargoes going to or coming from ports around the world—temptations for bloodthirsty pirates.

As is well known in pirate lore, the great buccaneers who once sailed the New Jersey waters always buried treasure for later retrieval. It was customary to murder at least one, if not all, of the crew that buried the treasure, and bury the body or bodies atop the treasure. The theory was that the vengeful ghost or ghosts thus created would guard the treasure against looters. Doubtless it also helped keep secret the burial spot if most witnesses were killed.

But pirates thirsted for more than blood and treasure. Like all sailors, they needed to land on occasion to replenish their supplies of fresh water. Not wanting to risk entering ports in search of water, the pirates preferred to land in isolated, uninhabited places to refill their water casks. A freshwater spring called the "spout" on Sandy Hook became a favorite of pirates, including the notorious Captain Kidd. Freshwater Lake Lily, at Cape May Point, was another pirate watering hole, at the opposite end of the Jersey shore. This too attracted Kidd's attention.

Woe to any local residents who might stumble into a pirate crew landing for water. Witnesses were killed immediately. It is widely believed that pirates sometimes buried treasure near their water sources, intending to dig them up again in the future. The usual suspects among pirates said to have left treasure in New Jersey include Jean Lafitte of New Orleans, Blackbeard (a.k.a. Edward Teach), and Captain Kidd. Alleged burial sites range along the seacoast from Sandy Hook to Cape May Point, and inland up the Delaware, Mullica, Maurice, Cohansey, and Great Egg Harbor Rivers. There are rumors of buried treasure on Sandy Hook, Money Island, Long Beach Island, and Cape May Point. As one story goes, Captain Kidd anchored near the mouth of Brigantine Inlet one summer day in 1698 and came ashore to bury his gold, which was stored in a heavy leather and brass-bound sea chest. Kidd and his first mate, Timothy Jones, later returned to dig up the chest and bury it in another spot. According to William McMahon in *South Jersey Towns*, "A fight ensued, and Jones was killed by Kidd, who buried his former mate beside the chest before departing. The alleged loot was never found."

So good luck hunting, but remember that you'll likely find human bones on top of the treasure chest.

Sailing Lore

New Jersey's coastline generated volumes of legends long before European immigrants settled by the water. Superstitions of the sea, as collected and categorized by David Pickering in the *Casell Dictionary of Superstitions,* are another rich vein of New Jersey folklore and belief. New Jersey, being a coastal state with many harbors, great and small, has a long history of sailors and fishermen. Those who are brave enough to go to sea share many superstitions about how to behave at sea, and how to read the signs of good or bad luck. The word *superstition* comes from a Latin word meaning soothsaying. Soothsayers foretold the future, and they were supposed to foretell it accurately, as *sooth* means the truth or reality.

For sailing ships, the Jersey coast was a dangerous place to be avoided at all cost; safe harbors were on the Hudson and Delaware Rivers. Ships need not only protected harbors, but also deep water alongside land, and these ships' requirements were not found between Sandy Hook on the north and Cape May to the south. The winds that carried ships across the seas could also smash them against the shore. Ships were safest either far at sea, where no land existed, or in deep-water harbors protecting them from storm waves. Sailing vessels tried to stay well off New Jersey's treacherously shallow shoreline of gentle beaches and deceptive inlets. But given the busy ports at either end of the Jersey shore, this hostile shore was not always easily avoided. Many ships in the vicinity, shoal waters, and frequent storms all added up to make this the graveyard of the Atlantic.

Those who made a living on the waves were very vulnerable, and as a result, they were interested in avoiding bad luck and inviting good luck. The superstitions familiar to many sailors and fishermen are ancient, but they are still observed today along the shores and on the waters of New Jersey.

If a crewmember or passenger died aboard ship, this was considered a very bad omen. By tradition, the body was carefully handled and disposed of, lest the ghost stay aboard. The corpse had to be laid parallel to the ship's keel, lengthwise not crosswise. The head had to be at the back, so that as the ghost rose from the body, it would face the bow, in the direction the ship was traveling. If the ship was more than a day from port, the body had to buried at sea. On a sailing ship, the corpse was sewn into a sail before being dumped overboard. The body was weighted so that it would sink before sharks were attracted.

It was believed that a ship should always be boarded right foot first, and from the ship's right (starboard) side. Although some old-timers thought that a woman aboard might bring bad luck, all agreed that a baby being born abroad brought good luck to that ship. When a ship embarked on its first voyage, an old shoe would be thrown into its wake, much like tying old shoes to the car of a couple departing on their honeymoon. Seasoned sailors tossed a penny overboard as their ship left its dock, tribute to Neptune, god of the sea. If Neptune didn't get his tribute, he might have seen to it that the ship never returned. Similarly, to guarantee a good catch, fishermen tossed a penny into the first net to be lowered to appease Neptune. Some said that tossing a little salt into the sea would produce a good catch. Many fishermen tossed back the first fish caught on the voyage to encourage Neptune to send more fish toward them. On a fishing boat's first voyage, however, the first fish caught was nailed to the mast.

A ship under construction was never called by its name. The name was officially known only at launching. For this reason, shipyards assign a number to "builds" or "hulls" under construction. The number refers to the hull's sequence among all boats or ships built there, as in "Hull 121" or "Build 97." Once named at launching, it was considered very bad luck to ever change the name. Even if a male name was given, a ship was always referred to as "she."

The custom of smashing a bottle of champagne against the bow of a ship, often called "christening," has its origins in a dark superstition of the Vikings. The ancient warriors always launched their longboats over the bodies of enemies or slaves so that the boat slid into the sea easily, having been lubricated by blood. A boat "born in blood" would have a long, lucky life, riding high over the waves. In less bloodthirsty times, red wine was substituted for blood, and eventually champagne was used. It is considered bad luck if the champagne bottle does not break on the first contact with the ship. To avoid such bad luck, experienced boat builders supply a bottle that has been scratched or incised in several places to encourage easy breaking.

European sailors believe that a cat aboard ship is good luck but two cats bring bad luck. If the cat falls overboard, the ship may be doomed. American sailors have mixed opinions on cats aboard ship; some think it is good luck but others think cats bring bad luck.

There are many seafarers' superstitions about birds. Bringing a live bird aboard is the worst luck. But if a bird lands on a ship at sea, it is usually good luck. If a land-based bird, like a sparrow or robin, lands aboard, it is an honored guest seeking refuge and brings good luck. An albatross, thought to contain a dead seaman's spirit, must never be killed. Its very appearance heralds a storm. Bird droppings on deck must not be removed until after the next storm, which will most likely remove them anyway. Sea gulls may bring bad luck; they are believed to contain the restless spirits of those drowned at sea. When gulls fly a long, straight line over the water, they are following a drowned man's spirit moving across the seabed. Though not welcomed, gulls must never be harmed. Truly superstitious sailors may believe that a seabird defecating on them is the best fortune of all.

Sea creatures also feature in many superstitions. A shark following a boat foretells a death aboard; three sharks trailing a boat practically guarantee impending death. Porpoises or dolphins are good news. Considered friendly to people, porpoises are said to welcome lucky ships into a harbor. Porpoises at play during a storm foretell a quick end to that storm. Whales generally are good omens, but seeing a whale in a place where they have not been seen before could be a bad omen. Seeing whales "out of season" (on New Jersey's coast, whales are "in season" during winter) could signify bad news.

If a fisherman, on his way to the harbor, comes across a member of the clergy, a cross-eyed person, or a woman wearing a white apron, he should go home and not board his vessel until the next tide. It is very unlucky to take the name of the Almighty in vain while at sea.

When building a ship, a silver coin must be placed under the base of a mast. Failure to do so will mean the mast will fall in a storm. It is bad luck to paint a ship green.

Davy Jones is an evil spirit believed to live at the bottom of the sea. It is thought that *Davy* is a West Indian voodoo name for the Devil, and that the Welsh surname Jones is derived from Jonah, the Biblical name that must never be given a future sailor or fisherman.

The End of an "Era"

In 1854, about four hundred eager immigrants set sail on the *New Era*, a ship that was supposed to carry them from Europe to their new homes in America. They traveled safely across the Atlantic Ocean but, with the town of Asbury Park in sight, became the victims of a sudden, violent storm. The ship, swamped by icy waves and brutal winds, was abruptly grounded off the coast. Rescue workers labored to bring as many passengers as possible to shore, using the newly invented life car system that reached the ship on a cable, but the *New Era* sank with almost two-thirds of the passengers still on board. When the weather cleared and rescue workers were able to board the ship, they soon discovered a sad truth: Many of the immigrants had turned their small savings into gold, which they had sewn into the lining of their clothes. This small amount of money, which would have been barely enough to help them start life over in a new land, had been sufficient to weigh them down and keep them from surfacing in the ship's hold, resulting in their untimely death. Their ghosts are said to wander along the beaches at night, jingling the gold coins that had kept them from swimming to safety.

That same year, the packet *Powhatan* went aground off the coast of Brigantine, sheared in two by the violence of a sudden storm. Local residents brought about forty bodies to shore and buried them at Rum Point, but many others were seen floating in the bay. Two brothers, Isaac and Robert Smith of Smithville, reportedly retrieved as many of the passengers as they could and buried them in a common grave in the old Quaker cemetery at Smithville. Travelers through the area have reported that a swirling white mist is periodically seen flowing around the cemetery, especially after a storm.

The Morro Castle Disaster

The last great maritime disaster along the Jersey shore happened on Friday night, September 7, 1934. The fast modern liner *Morro Castle*, returning to New York from a cruise to Havana, Cuba, mysteriously caught fire. Fire swept through the ship uncontrollably, and the powerless hulk drifted ashore just off Asbury Park's Convention Hall the next morning. Hundreds died in the fire or drowned after jumping off the burning ship in a panic at sea. Corpses washed ashore from Sea Girt northward, and many beach communities have been the sites of ghostly apparitions along the beaches ever since.

Asbury Park especially is said to be haunted by fire-scarred ghosts, made particulary vindictive by the fact that the local merchants made a killing from the tragedy. The fire-blackened, still-smoldering death ship lay beached yards away from the town's boardwalk. Ghoulish crowds came to gawk at the hulk so conveniently close to shore, and local merchants had their best days in history. A record 150,000 viewed the *Morro Castle*. The terrible incident became a moneymaker for the town. In what may still hold the New Jersey record for a traffic jam, rubberneckers caused a monumental backup all the way from Asbury Park to the Holland Tunnel. While the dead were still being dragged off the beaches, Asbury Park businesspeople were gleefully hurrying to their banks with large and unexpected deposits.

Few remembered that Asbury Park's newspaper, the *Daily Spray,* fifty years earlier had actually wished for exactly this kind of disaster. As cited in Hal Burton's *Morro Castle* book, an 1884 editorial declared, "We need a first-class shipwreck . . . to make Asbury Park a famous winter resort. The unlucky ship should strike head-on and we could accommodate her all winter."

The city of Asbury Park actually considered claiming the abandoned ship and keeping her there as a permanent tourist attraction. The wreck wasn't towed away until March of the following year. It took half a century, but Asbury Park's wish for a moneymaking wreck was eerily fulfilled.

The Ghosts of Barnegat

A handsome couple, appearing to be in their thirties, strolls down the streets of the small resort town of Barnegat Light. They are singing softly, an old nineteenth-century sentimental song called "In the Sweet Bye and Bye," a song often sung softly as a lullaby in days past. This scene usually takes place around 7 or 8 P.M., when a small child might be placed in its bed for the night. But why is the couple always dressed in antique winter clothing—heavy coats, scarves, gloves, and hats—even in the heat of summer?

Because they are ghosts. The strolling couple are singing a lullaby to their baby daughter, who was separated from her parents as a result of a late nineteenth-century shipwreck, when the schooner *Tolck* ran aground near Barnegat Light on a stormy night in January.

When the *Tolck* was driven onto a sandbar offshore, the lifesaving service sprang into action. As was customary in those days, a grappling hook attached to a line was fired at the stranded vessel by a specially designed gun. Once fastened securely to the endangered ship, this line was used to send an iron life car, a kind of human-size hollow torpedo, out to the ship. In this way, the crew could be rescued one or two at a time, carried to safety above the storm waves, hauled back snug in the life car.

But the ship's owner and captain refused to leave. He was honoring an old tradition that the captain was last to leave, if indeed he left at all. There was a practical reason behind this tradition. An abandoned ship could be claimed as salvage by anyone who succeeded in towing her into harbor. The captain could not afford to abandon his ship, which represented all his savings. He had a wife and infant daughter to support, so he lashed himself to a mast to ride out the storm. After all, his iron-hulled schooner did not appear to be breaking up. His wife, also aboard on this ill-fated voyage, insisted on staying with him but decided to send her child ashore in the arms of the first mate. "Pray that we do not drown!" she begged the first mate. "But see that our child is safe!"

They didn't drown; the *Tolck* did indeed remain intact through the storm. But the captain and his wife were discovered the next morning—frozen to death in each other's arms. Their baby, entrusted to a local family, survived and grew up within sight of the place where her parents had perished. But on stormy nights ever since, the captain and his lady walk the streets, singing a lullaby to their daughter, hoping she'll hear it and be reassured of her parents' undying love.

The Woman in White

Is it any wonder that the spirits of the dead continue to wander along the beaches? They had died before their time, victims of callous greed, and in sight of the shore.

Often mislabeled as pirates, wreckers caused their share of heartbreak by causing shipwrecks along the shore during those years. Many legends were born from these shipwrecks, but few are as tragic as the story of the Woman in White, who is said to haunt the Jersey shore even today. Over the years, two versions of the story have been documented. The first, set on Long Beach Island, involved the beautiful daughter of a man who captained a crew of wreckers. The young woman was in love with a sailor, who was not due to return from his next voyage until the end of the summer. One warm night, she joined her father and his crew in setting up lanterns to draw an unsuspecting ship toward the shore. After it crashed, the cargo and the bodies of the crew and passengers began to wash up along the beach. The young woman went eagerly to

work with the rest of the murderous crew, gathering fine goods and robbing the dead of their jewelry.

As she approached the battered body of one man, however, her anticipation turned to horror. It was her sailor. He had missed her so badly that he returned early from his voyage on another ship. Driven mad with grief and guilt, the young woman afterward spent long, lonely days on that same stretch of beach, waiting for her lover's ship to appear on the horizon. Brokenhearted, she died not long afterward, and her spirit continues to be seen late at night or on mist-filled mornings, walking anxiously along the shore.

In 1895, noted American author Stephen Crane documented another version of the Woman in White. The story was one of a number of such ghostly tales he wrote about the New Jersey shore while working as a reporter for the *New York Press*. In Crane's version, the legend started in 1815 in the tiny fishing village of Metedeconk, on the mainland side of Barnegat Bay. According to Crane, the story began with a gorgeous young lady who was in love with the captain of a sailing ship, who left her three times a year to go off on extensive voyages. Such sea trips were highly prosperous, and the young man was determined to make his fortune before he settled down.

However, the young woman grew tired of waiting and quarreled with her lover just before he left on a voyage to Buenos Aires in South America. Although he swore his undying love, she turned away, but became immediately regretful as the ship set sail. The woman began to mourn as his ship left the harbor, and in the days that followed, she hovered on the beach, waiting and watching for a familiar sail to return from the southeast.

One night, a violent storm broke as she stood at the water's edge. To her dismay, flashing lights suddenly appeared through the dark from the ocean, warning those on land that an approaching ship was in trouble. As the ship drew closer, sailors could be seen leaping overboard, but they were not able to swim to shore through the crashing surf. As the tragedy unfolded before her, the young woman glanced down to see a body tossed almost at her feet by a massive wave. It was her sea captain—finally returning from his voyage. Like the young woman on Long Beach Island, she went mad with grief and died soon afterward.

In the years that followed, Crane recounted, fishermen from the village told tales of a spectral figure haunting the beaches after dark. One fisherman, returning from the sea late one night, allegedly encountered the ghost, whom Crane described as "the white lady": "Her hair fell in disheveled masses over her shoulders, her hands were clasped appealingly, and her large eyes gleamed with the one eternal and dread interrogation." With a cry of terror, the fisherman ran all the way home before she could ask if he had seen her lover, the captain. Today many fishermen choose to bring their nets in well before dark—perhaps to avoid an uncomfortable encounter with New Jersey's mysterious and terrifying Woman in White.

Haunts of the Supernatural

MANY GHOSTHUNTERS AND THOUGHTFUL COLLECTORS OF GHOST STORIES have observed that there seems to be a geography of hauntings, ghost appearances, and other supernatural activity. Hot spots for ghost stories exist where ghostly activity seems to be concentrated. While individual spirits typically are confined to a specific building, or even a room or two, some regions seem to have many such ghosts, whereas other areas have few or none. Wandering ghosts, who appear to move about a less confined area than a house or graveyard, likewise are common in some areas, rare in others.

As documented in this book, two of the most haunted regions of New Jersey are the northwest Highlands and South Jersey's Pinelands. What, if anything, do these areas have in common other than an apparent attractiveness or hospitality to ghosts? In terrain, they are opposites—the flat, sandy Pinelands and the steep, rugged hills of the Highlands. Neither is particularly productive farmland, but for different reasons.

But there is something in common—something that other parts of the Garden State lack. That something is iron ore and a history of iron mining, smelting, and working. Is there a clue here? Alone among the metals, only iron can be magnetized. Only iron is used in compasses to point the way to the magnetic North Pole. Our understanding of the relationships among magnetism and electricity is only about two centuries old. We have concluded that the earth produces a global magnetic field, which is why compass needles reliably point to the poles of this field.

There was a time—in fact, a long time in human history—when magnetic compass needles seemed every bit as mysterious and inexplicable as ghosts. People knew compasses worked, but not why and how.

Many ghost stories mention the ghost's influence on electric lights and appliances. Lights flick off or on without any apparent cause, other than the presence of a ghost.

Do ghostly apparitions cause magnetic fields that can affect electricity? Or are ghosts somehow a result of magnetic fields? Or perhaps both? Surely this is a line of inquiry worth pursuing by ghosthunters. And it might explain the unusual frequency of hauntings in both the Highlands and the Pinelands of New Jersey.

Ghostly Guidelines

Famous New Jersey ghosthunter Virginia Joslin has developed a list of "Guidelines for Ghosthunters" based on her many experiences in the field. This is what you may experience upon moving into a haunted house. Joslin emphasizes that these happenings are typical when a normal, non-ghost-oriented family moves into a house occupied by a restless spirit or two. Hypersensitive people may recognize the signs of a haunting sooner, and in more severe form.

Generally, ghosts do not immediately announce their presence to a typical family. Characteristically, the new arrivals are not aware of, or sensitized to, their resident spirit or spirits until after about six months. The first sign of a haunting usually takes the form of footsteps heard where and when no living person could have caused them. Dogs or cats may show awareness of spirits before people do, becoming frightened or alarmed, acting strangely without any obvious cause. According to Joslin, those mysterious footsteps never just amble about; they repeatedly begin and end at specific locations.

The most common timing of ghostly happenings is not, contrary to legend, midnight. Dawn and dusk are most frequent, but manifestations of spirits can happen at any times.

If major architectural changes are made to the property in question, such as windows or doors being sealed over or newly created, or walls torn out or built, the resident ghosts may either leave permanently or may stay and ignore the change. The human occupants may notice that ghostly footsteps appear to move through walls that once were pierced by a door, or a now nonexistent door may be heard to open and close as though still there.

If the architecture of a building shows unplanned flaws or imbalances—such as sloping floors, windows out of line with others, or uneven spacing of support beams—this may signify a haunted house. Joslin emphasized that houses never are haunted all over—mysterious appearances, sounds, and the like are confined to a room or two, or one floor but not another.

If a poltergeist is present, causing physical objects to move without rational explanation, no person will be hit by flying objects, though near misses are common.

Commonly, there is a cold spot at the center of the spiritual manifestations. The temperature there will be noticeably colder than the rest of the building, sometimes bitterly cold.

If the ghost in question is in fact a deceased family member, the visual or auditory manifestation may be accompanied by a distinctive aroma or odor. Flowers, perfume, fresh bread, tobacco, chocolate, or sweat are common ghostly odors.

Electric lights or small electrical appliances may be affected by, apparently, electrical fields associated with the spirit. These lights or appliances may function aberrantly, not malfunction. For example, lights may go out or come on a fraction of a second before a person touches the switch. Lights or appliances may suddenly shut off without any human touch.

Investigating the Supernatural

For almost two centuries, Americans have taken an avid interest in supernatural research. Some have approached the topic with skepticism, determined to "bust" any ghosts they might find. Others are more concerned with simply gathering knowledge about the paranormal in order to increase understanding of the subject. Still others are interested in the excitement of "forbidden fruits"—going into unknown and often forbidden territory to find what lurks beyond.

In recent years, there has been a renaissance of interest in the field of parapsychology. Whether it is because we seem to live in increasingly troubled times or because technology no longer provides the answers we seek, many people are determined to learn more about the supernatural. Some New Jersey residents have formed organizations to increase their resources and areas of study. One such organization, incorporated in January 2002, is South Jersey Paranormal Research (SJPR), a Gloucester Township group. Susan Bove, a co-director of SJPR, and Lois Weber, a field investigator, are just two of the members who participate in field investigations, which are offered free of charge to the public.

Both women had grown up in households that were open-minded enough to accept the existence of ghosts. As a result, Bove developed an interest in the supernatural that ultimately led to the formation of SJPR. Weber got involved with the organization shortly after she retired.

"My husband said I should find something to do that I would really love, and I said I would love to be involved with the paranormal," she recalled. "The next day, there was article in the newspaper about SJPR. It was fate. It was kismet. So I joined."

Weber and Bove quickly became good friends through their shared passion for the work. Although not all members are required to get actively involved in field investigations, those who do are required to undergo rigorous testing to make sure they will react calmly in the face of any supernatural phenomena. Once they have participated in two cemetery sightings and two indoor sightings, and have filed the necessary reports, they can continue to investigate any reports that are brought to the group's attention. Weber liked the idea of being on the scene and recording spectral sightings with videos and audiotapes that are added to SJPR's growing research library.

The two women agreed that the most unusual investigation they ever participated in involved the girl who liked to sing in the Masonic Lodge in Woodbury. Weber, who does a lot of work on the group's recordings, has audio recordings of the night the investigators first "met" the lively spirit. She remembered: "Susan was on the second floor, I was on the third floor. I was leaning over the railing, looking down because there was nothing going on. All of a sudden, I could hear a woman singing loudly—it was coming from the second floor and echoing through the building. Immediately, everybody's on the radio going, 'Did you hear that?! Did you hear that?!'"

The woman continued singing several more songs, although Weber says she only heard her twice. As she moved cautiously down to the second floor, she asked, "If you're a woman, what are you doing in the lodge?" It seemed a logical question, since the Masons are an all-male organization. Although she didn't hear an immediate answer, when she was checking her audiotapes later, Weber discovered that another woman's spirit had responded to her question. She clearly heard a second woman's voice answer in an "isn't it obvious" tone: "Singing. She likes to sing."

The mystery woman has been heard in the lodge on other occasions and has played cat and mouse with the investigators—every time they entered a room, she moved on to the next. Some research on the part of the investigators eventually revealed that there had been a sister organization to the Masonic Lodge. Women were permitted to use the building for musical entertainment and other activities. Bove said the ghosts may have lived around the 1920s, from the type of music the investigators heard.

In another investigation, SJPR members paid several visits to a house in Haddon Township that seemed to be the site of a variety of spectral activity.

"The residents' daughter actually has four children that she plays with who are spirits," Bove said. "She says they come in through the window. The mother will go to the daughter's door, and she'll hear her daughter playing in there—like she's interacting with other kids. When we went in there, not only did we hear little girls and a little boy, but we have them on audio, too."

On a different occasion, Bove recalled, "The whole night we were there, down in the living room, all these little lights kept dancing across the TV screen, even though the TV was off."

Surprisingly enough, although the investigators were excited by the activity, the homeowner appeared blasé.

"She was used to it," Bove said. "She could be vacuuming, and she'd look up and see a little boy standing there."

A later review of the audiotapes revealed the voice of a little girl named Mary, repeatedly exclaiming, "Did you see it?!" in reference to the lights on the TV screen. Through research, they later learned that a Mary Keegan had once lived across the street and frequently visited the house to play with her cousins.

During that same evening, investigators heard a loud bang echo from the grandfather clock that the resident's father had made. Apparently, the weight on the pendulum had fallen off and crashed to the bottom of the case, but it would have been physically impossible for the weight to have fallen on its own. When investigators later checked the videotapes of that night's work, the swirling lights that had played across the television were visible around the clock right before the crash.

In addition to investigations, SJPR hosts educational seminars on supernatural activities that are open to the public. Anyone interested in learning more about the nonprofit organization can visit their website at www.sjpr.com.

Another organization that has been working in the field is South Jersey Ghost Research (SJGR), a professional research group organized by director David Juliano. SJGR includes members who formerly worked with Ghost Hunters of America, an organization that traces its roots back to 1955. In addition to conducting field investigations into the supernatural, members focus on educating the public about paranormal phenomena. Also a nonprofit agency, SJGR has researched spectral sightings in New Jersey, eastern Pennsylvania, Delaware, and New York City.

Juliano, who conducts field investigations at least once a week, feels that the most interesting investigation he has participated in was held at Burlington County Jail in 1999. The SJGR team documented evidence of supernatural activity, including a presence reported in Joseph Clough's death-row cell long after it was no longer used. They also heard voices and screams coming from various points of the building and found a single bare footprint in the former shower stalls. During the investigation, motion detectors recorded movement, and videotape footage shows orbs in motion at the same time. Juliano recalled that the team also recorded a man's voice declaring, "Go out there," at the exact moment the orbs appeared. For more information on SJGR, visit the group's website at www.sjgr.org.

Other New Jersey groups that investigate supernatural activity include the New Jersey Ghost Hunters Society, based in Chatham (www.njghs.net) and the New Jersey Ghost Research organization, located in Turnersville (www.njghostresearch.org).

Ghost Tours in the Garden State

A NUMBER OF NEW JERSEY CITIES AND TOWNS HAVE BEGUN OFFERING "ghost tours," following the lead of New Orleans, where they have been a tradition for many years. Not every town offers actual "ghost tours," however, so you might want to consider planning your own to some of the unique locations that exist in the Garden State. Here are some suggestions. Burlington Country's Mount Misery, originally named Mount Miseracorde by the French land speculator Peter Bard, was a small town about fifteen miles southeast of Mount Holly. It consisted of about five houses, a sawmill, and a tavern. Burlington County was once the home of Purgatory as well, another village that is no longer on the map. Jenny Jump State Forest in Hope is home to both Shades of Death Road and Ghost Lake. Atlantic County has a rural Route 666 that looks like just another country road by day, but no one willingly travels it by night. Then there are Hell's Kitchen, Double Trouble, and Bone Hill. Although you won't find Hell's Kitchen and Bone Hill on a modern New Jersey map, Double Trouble is located a few miles south of Toms River on the eastern coast.

For those who enjoy a more formal introduction to local haunts, Ocean City and Cape May give visitors the opportunity to "meet" some of the colorful characters who once lived in those shore communities. Ocean City's tour guides include a stop at the famous Flanders Hotel, a popular 1920s seaside establishment. Although most visitors rarely associate ghosts with the family resort, the Flanders has a resident spirit named Emily. Simon Lake, one of the town's founding fathers, is another ghost, who supposedly appears whenever there is any discussion about removing Ocean City's ban on alcohol.

Other towns often offer similar tours during the fall as a way of promoting local history. Another type of day trip that has become popular in recent years is the "cemetery tour," where hardy people troop to different graveyards to learn more about the lives of the people who are buried there—and perhaps see a ghostly sighting or two. In Cranbury, area residents claim that on stormy nights right around Halloween, you can hear the fatal stagecoach crash where the Philadelphia merchant William Christie was killed. The incident occurred directly across the street from the First Presbyterian Church graveyard.

There are cemeteries from the northernmost reaches of the state down to the southern seashore where local residents claim that spirits walk. Since dates and companies are changeable, it would be virtually impossible to offer a listing of all ghost tours here. If you are interested in visiting a particular area, we suggest you contact the local Chamber of Commerce or spend some time on the Internet for the latest information on regional folklore. Sites like www.hauntfinder.com and www.horrorfind.com offer a wide selection of "spirited" activities, ranging from the Hollowgraves Haunted Manor, open all summer at the Keansburg Amusement Park, to the Screaming Run Haunted Walk, held around Halloween at Leaming's Run Gardens in Swainton.

Getting Weird in the Garden State

ONE EXCELLENT RESOURCE FOR THE LATEST NEWS OF THE SUPERNATURAL is *Weird New Jersey*, a fascinating publication that began to pique the imagination of readers with tales of the supernatural in 1989, when it first appeared in newsletter form. Since that time, Mark Sceurman and Mark Moran, who describe themselves as the "publishers, editors, everything" of *WNJ*, have produced nine issues— one per year—that have attracted an ever-growing audience.

Weird New Jersey is promoted as "your travel guide to New Jersey's local legends and best kept secrets," and it does an excellent job of covering the paranormal. Many of the articles are sent in by readers who are audacious enough to explore underground tunnels, abandoned sanitariums, and other unusual places in hope of sighting a spectral presence. *Weird New Jersey*, which plays a valuable role in documenting modern-day folk tales and keeping them alive for future generations, can also be found on the Internet at www.weirdnj.com.

The Weird Wide Web

Anyone who has access to the Internet knows that you can find just about anything with a few keystrokes, regardless of the subject. If you are interested in learning more about New Jersey's haunted history, there are thousands of sites devoted to the supernatural, ranging from contemporary and historical horror tales to practical advice on casting your own magical spells. Whether or not you do that voodoo, a number of them include stories about the paranormal in New Jersey and are ideal for the armchair adventurer who would rather not confront any ghosts or goblins firsthand. If you're interested in exploring, here are just a few stops on the Internet that are worth visiting:

www.paranormalnews.com
www.realhaunts.com
www.theshadowlands.net
www.njghs.net
www.ghostvillage.com
www.lonestarspirits.org

Bibliography

Adams, Charles J. III *Atlantic County Ghost Stories*. Reading, PA: Exeter House Books, 2003.

Barber, John, and Henry Howe. *Historical Collections of the State of New Jersey*. New York: S. Tuttle, 1844.

Beck, Henry Charlton. *Forgotten Towns of Southern New Jersey*. New Brunswick, NJ: Rutgers University Press, 1961.

———. *The Roads of Home: Lanes and Legends of New Jersey*. New Brunswick, NJ: Rutgers University Press, 1956.

———. *Tales and Towns of Northern New Jersey*. New Brunswick, NJ: Rutgers University Press, 1964.

Botkin, B. A., ed. *A Treasury of American Folklore*. New York: Crown Publishers, 1944.

Burton, Hal. *Morro Castle*. New York: Viking Press, 1973.

Cavnar, Valerie Barnes. *The Strange and Mysterious Past in the Somerset Hills Area*. Bernardsville, NJ: Bernardsville Book Company, 1975.

Chalmers, Kathryn H. *Down the Long-A-Coming*. Moorestown, NJ: News Chronicle, 1951.

Cohen, David Steven. *The Folklore and Folklife of New Jersey*. New Brunswick, NJ: Rutgers University Press, 1984.

———. *The Ramapo Mountain People*. New Brunswick, NJ: Rutgers University Press, 1974.

Cross, Dorothy. *New Jersey's Indians*. Trenton, NJ: New Jersey State Museum, 1976.

Forbes, B. C. "Edison Working on How to Communicate with the Next World." *American Magazine* (October 1920).

Gordon, Thomas F. *The History of New Jersey from Its Discovery by Europeans to the Adoption of the Federal Constitution*. Trenton, NJ: Daniel Fenton, Publisher, 1861.

Holzer, Hans. *Yankee Ghosts*. Indianapolis: Bobbs Merrill, 1963.

Jahn, Robert. *Down Barnegat Bay: A Nor'easter Midnight Reader*. Mantaloking, NJ: Beachcomber Press, 1980.

Johnson, Eileen Luz, comp. *Phyllis: The Library Ghost.* Newark, NJ: John-ston Letter Co., 1991.

———. Interview in the *Trenton Times,* November 16, 1966.

Joslin, Virginia, ed. *Ghosts of Gloucester County.* Woodbury, NJ: Gloucester County Cultural and Heritage Commission, 1982.

Krantz, Les. *America by Numbers: Facts and Figures from the Weighty to the Way-Out.* Boston: Houghton Mifflin, 1993.

Leap, William W. *The History of Runnemede New Jersey, 1626–1976.* Runnemede, NJ: Borough of Runnemede, 1981.

Mappen, Marc. *Jerseyana: The Underside of New Jersey History.* New Brunswick, NJ: Rutgers University Press, 1992.

McCloy, James F., and Ray Miller Jr. *The Jersey Devil.* Moorestown, NJ: Middle Atlantic Press, 1976.

McMahon, William. *Historic South Jersey Towns.* Atlantic City, NJ: Press Publishing Company, 1964.

———. *South Jersey Towns: History and Legend.* New Brunswick, NJ: Rutgers University Press, 1973.

Mills, W. Jay. *Historic Houses of New Jersey.* Union City, NJ: William H. Wise & Co., 1977.

Moore, W. Clement. "The White Stag of Shamong." *Basto Citizens Committee Gazette* (spring/summer 1993): 2.

Nelson, William, ed. *Documents Relating to the Colonial History of the State of New Jersey.* Vol. 11. Paterson, NJ: The Press Printing and Publishing Co., 1894.

Pickering, David. *Casell Dictionary of Superstitions.* London: Casell, 1995.

Raum, John O. *The History of New Jersey.* Philadelphia: John E. Potter and Company, 1877.

Skinner, Charles M. *American Myths and Legends.* Detroit: Gale Research Company, 1974.

Stockton, Frank R. *Stories of New Jersey.* New Brunswick, NJ: Rutgers University Press, 1991.

Wilson, Harold F. *The Jersey Shore: A Social and Economic History of the Counties of Atlantic, Cape May, Monmouth and Ocean.* New York: Lewis Historical Publishing Company, 1953.

Acknowledgments

WE WISH TO THANK OUR SKILLFUL EDITOR, KYLE WEAVER, FOR HIS enthusiastic support and encouragement. His assistant, Amy Cooper, diligently attended to numerous details during the books production. The wonderfully atmospheric illustrations are an important contribution to this book; they are the work of a talented young artist named Heather Adel.

This book is dedicated with love to my mother, Rose Siciliano Martinelli, who inspires me daily with her compassion and her sense of humor, and to my late father, Franklin A. Martinelli, who created his music on a different kind of keyboard. Thank you both for everything.

I am grateful for the continuing support and patience of Mary Ann and Jim Larro, Denise Dendrinos, Janet Peterson, Ruth and Hartley Tucker, and other friends and family members who believed even when I doubted. In addition, I would like to thank Susan Bove and Lois Weber, David Juliano, and others who preferred to keep their identities confidential for sharing their close encounters with the supernatural. I appreciate the assistance of Douglas Tarr, of the National Park Service; Maud Thiebaud, a local history room volunteer at Bernardsville Public Library; and the Reverend J. R. "Doc" Gearl, who were invaluable resources during the research process. Finally, I will always be especially grateful to the staff of Vineland Public Library, who unfailingly produced obscure texts through the magic of interlibrary loan, helping to make this book a reality.

Patricia A. Martinelli

I dedicate this book to my beloved sons, Wayne Charles Stansfield and Paul Scott Stansfield, who, though skeptics on some matters, are steadfast believers in honor, fidelity, and family.

I wish to thank my many friends and colleagues at the Campbell Library of Rowan University for their professional knowledge and many personal courtesies. Foremost among these always helpful and unfailingly friendly colleagues are Maryann Gonzalez, Joyce Olsen, and William Garrabrant of the Stewart Room and Assistant Director Greg Potter. They expertly tracked down sources ranging from eighteenth-century books on witchcraft to newspaper back files, and even supplied a few ghost stories of their own.

Good friends Bill and Jill Top of Hove, England, shared their horrific personal experiences in a haunted cottage, thus unknowingly planting the seed of a long fascination with ghost stories. Many friends and colleagues, and even a relative here and there, shared their ghost stories, many on the grounds of anonymity. They know who they are and know I appreciate their interest in our project.

Charles A. Stansfield Jr.